THE ANNOTATED LUTHER STUDY EDITION

The Small Catechism

1529

THE ANNOTATED LUTHER STUDY EDITION

The Small Catechism, 1529

TIMOTHY J. WENGERT

Mary Jane Haemig
EDITOR

Fortress Press
Minneapolis

The Small Catechism, 1529
THE ANNOTATED LUTHER STUDY EDITION

Excerpted from The Annotated Luther, Volume 4, *Pastoral Writings* (Minneapolis: Fortress Press, 2016), Mary Jane Haemig, volume editor.

Fortress Press Publication Staff:
Scott Tunseth, Project Editor
Alicia Ehlers, Production Manager
Laurie Ingram, Cover Design
Michael Moore, Permissions

Copyeditor: David Lott
Series design and typesetting: Ann Delgehausen, Trio Bookworks
Proofreader: Paul Kobelski, The HK Scriptorium

Library of Congress Cataloging-in-Publication Data is available

Print ISBN: 978-1-5064-3247-2
eISBN: 978-1-5064-3248-9

The paper used in this publication meets the minimum requirements of American National Standard for Information Sciences—Permanence of Paper for Printed Library Materials, ANSI Z329, 48-1984.

Manufactured in the U.S.A.

Contents

Publisher's Note

About the Annotated Luther Study Edition

The volumes in The Annotated Luther Study Edition series have first been published in one of the comprehensive volumes of The Annotated Luther series. A description of that series and the volumes can be found in the Series Introduction (p. vii). While each comprehensive Annotated Luther volume can easily be used in classroom settings, we also recognize that treatises are often assigned individually for reading and study. To facilitate classroom and group use, we have pulled key treatises along with their introductions, annotations, and images directly from The Annotated Luther series volumes.

Please note that the study edition page numbers match the page numbers of the larger Annotated Luther volume in which it first appeared. We have intentionally retained the same page numbering to facilitate use of the study editions and larger volumes side by side.

The Small Catechism, 1529,
was first published in The Annotated Luther series,
Volume 4, *Pastoral Writings* (2016).

Series Introduction

Engaging the Essential Luther

Even after five hundred years Martin Luther continues to engage and challenge each new generation of scholars and believers alike. With 2017 marking the five-hundredth anniversary of Luther's *95 Theses*, Luther's theology and legacy are being explored around the world with new questions and methods and by diverse voices. His thought invites ongoing examination, his writings are a staple in classrooms and pulpits, and he speaks to an expanding assortment of conversation partners who use different languages and hale from different geographical and social contexts.

The six volumes of The Annotated Luther edition offer a flexible tool for the global reader of Luther, making many of his most important writings available in the *lingua franca* of our times as one way of facilitating interest in the Wittenberg reformer. They feature new introductions, annotations, revised translations, and textual notes, as well as visual enhancements (illustrations, art, photos, maps, and timelines). The Annotated Luther edition embodies Luther's own cherished principles of communication. Theological writing, like preaching, needs to reflect human beings' lived experience, benefits from up-to-date scholarship, and should be easily accessible to all. These volumes are designed to help teachers and students, pastors and laypersons, and other professionals in ministry understand the context in which the documents were written, recognize how the documents have shaped Protestant and Lutheran thinking, and interpret the meaning of these documents for faith and life today.

The Rationale for This Edition

For any reader of Luther, the sheer number of his works presents a challenge. Well over one hundred volumes comprise the scholarly edition of Luther's works, the so-called Weimar Ausgabe (WA), a publishing enterprise begun in 1883 and only completed in the twenty-first century. From 1955 to 1986, fifty-five volumes came to make up *Luther's Works* (American Edition) (LW), to which Concordia Publishing House, St. Louis, is adding still more. This English-language contribution to Luther studies, matched by similar translation projects for Erasmus of Rotterdam and John Calvin, provides a theological and historical gold mine for those interested in studying Luther's thought. But even these volumes are not always easy to use and are hardly portable. Electronic forms have increased availability, but preserving Luther in book form and providing readers with manageable selections are also important goals.

Moreover, since the publication of the WA and the first fifty-five volumes of the LW, research on the Reformation in general and on Martin Luther in particular has broken new ground and evolved, as has knowledge regarding the languages in which Luther wrote. Up-to-date information from a variety of sources is brought together in The Annotated Luther, building on the work done by previous generations of scholars. The language and phrasing of the translations have also been updated to reflect modern English usage. While the WA and, in a derivative way, LW remain the central source for Luther scholarship, the present critical and annotated English translation facilitates research internationally and invites a new generation of readers for whom Latin and German might prove an unsurpassable obstacle to accessing Luther. The WA provides the basic Luther texts (with some exceptions); the LW provides the basis for almost all translations.

Defining the "Essential Luther"

Deciding which works to include in this collection was not easy. Criteria included giving attention to Luther's initial key works; considering which publications had the most impact in his day and later; and taking account of Luther's own favorites, texts addressing specific issues of continued importance for today, and Luther's exegetical works. Taken as a whole, these works present the many sides of Luther, as reformer, pastor, biblical interpreter, and theologian. To serve today's readers and by using categories similar to those found in volumes 31–47 of Luther's works (published by Fortress Press), the volumes offer in the main a thematic rather than strictly chronological approach to Luther's writings. The volumes in the series include:

> Volume 1: *The Roots of Reform* (Timothy J. Wengert, editor)
> Volume 2: *Word and Faith* (Kirsi I. Stjerna, editor)
> Volume 3: *Church and Sacraments* (Paul W. Robinson, editor)
> Volume 4: *Pastoral Writings* (Mary Jane Haemig, editor)
> Volume 5: *Christian Life in the World* (Hans J. Hillerbrand, editor)
> Volume 6: *The Interpretation of Scripture* (Euan K. Cameron, editor)

The History of the Project

In 2011 Fortress Press convened an advisory board to explore the promise and parameters of a new English edition of Luther's essential works. Board members Denis Janz, Robert Kolb, Peter Matheson, Christine Helmer, and Kirsi Stjerna deliberated with

Fortress Press publisher Will Bergkamp to develop a concept and identify contributors. After a review with scholars in the field, college and seminary professors, and pastors, it was concluded that a single-language edition was more desirable than dual-language volumes.

In August 2012, Hans Hillerbrand, Kirsi Stjerna, and Timothy Wengert were appointed as general editors of the series with Scott Tunseth from Fortress Press as the project editor. The general editors were tasked with determining the contents of the volumes and developing the working principles of the series. They also helped with the identification and recruitment of additional volume editors, who in turn worked with the general editors to identify volume contributors. Mastery of the languages and unique knowledge of the subject matter were key factors in identifying contributors. Most contributors are North American scholars and native English speakers, but The Annotated Luther includes among its contributors a circle of international scholars. Likewise, the series is offered for a global network of teachers and students in seminary, university, and college classes, as well as pastors, lay teachers, and adult students in congregations seeking background and depth in Lutheran theology, biblical interpretation, and Reformation history.

Editorial Principles

The volume editors and contributors have, with few exceptions, used the translations of LW as the basis of their work, retranslating from the WA for the sake of clarity and contemporary usage. Where the LW translations have been substantively altered, explanatory notes have often been provided. More importantly, contributors have provided marginal notes to help readers understand theological and historical references. Introductions have been expanded and sharpened to reflect the very latest historical and theological research. In citing the Bible, care has been taken to reflect the German and Latin texts commonly used in the sixteenth century rather than modern editions, which often employ textual sources that were unavailable to Luther and his contemporaries.

Finally, all pieces in The Annotated Luther have been revised in the light of modern principles of inclusive language. This is not always an easy task with a historical author, but an intentional effort has been made to revise language throughout, with creativity and editorial liberties, to allow Luther's theology to speak free from unnecessary and unintended gender-exclusive language. This important principle provides an opportunity to translate accurately certain gender-neutral German and Latin expressions that Luther employed—for example, the Latin word *homo* and the German *Mensch* mean "human being," not simply "males." Using the words *man* and *men* to translate such terms would create an ambiguity not present in the original texts. The focus is on linguistic accuracy and Luther's intent. Regarding creedal formulations and trinitarian language, Luther's own expressions have been preserved, without entering the complex and important contemporary debates over language for God and the Trinity.

The 2017 anniversary of the publication of the *95 Theses* is providing an opportunity to assess the substance of Luther's role and influence in the Protestant Reformation. Revisiting Luther's essential writings not only allows reassessment of Luther's rationale and goals but also provides a new look at what Martin Luther was about and why new generations would still wish to engage him. We hope these six volumes offer a compelling invitation.

Hans J. Hillerbrand
Kirsi I. Stjerna
Timothy J. Wengert
General Editors

Abbreviations

AWA	Archiv für die Weimarer Ausgabe
BC	*The Book of Concord*, ed. Robert Kolb and Timothy J. Wengert (Minneapolis: Fortress Press, 2000)
Brecht	Martin Brecht, *Martin Luther*, trans. James L. Schaaf, 3 vols. (Philadelphia and Minneapolis: Fortress Press, 1985–1993)
CA	Augsburg Confession
CSEL	*Corpus scriptorum ecclesiasticorum latinorum*
LC	*The Large Catechism*
LW	*Luther's Works* [American edition], ed. Helmut Lehmann and Jaroslav Pelikan, 55 vols. (Philadelphia: Fortress Press; St. Louis: Concordia, 1955–86)
MLStA	*Martin Luther: Studienausgabe*, ed. Hans-Ulrich Delius, 6 vols. (Berlin and Leipzig: Evangelische Verlagsanstalt, 1979–99)
MPG	*Patrologiae cursus completus, series Graeca*, ed. Jacques-Paul Migne, 166 vols. (Paris, 1857–1866)
MPL	*Patrologiae cursus completus, series Latina*, ed. Jacques-Paul Migne, 217 vols. (Paris, 1844–1864)
ODCC	*The Oxford Dictionary of the Christian Church*, ed. F. L. Cross, 3rd ed. rev., ed. E. A. Livingstone (Oxford: Oxford University Press, 2005)
OER	*Oxford Encyclopedia of the Reformation*, ed. Hans J. Hillerbrand, 4 vols. (New York and Oxford: Oxford University Press, 1996)
SA	*The Smalcald Articles*
SC	*The Small Catechism*
SD	*Solid Declaration*
TAL	The Annotated Luther
VD	*Verzeichnis der im deutschen Sprachbereich erschienenen Drucke des Jahrhunderts* (Munich: Bayerische Staatsbibliothek; Herzog August Bibliothek in Wolfenbüttel, Stuttgart: Hiersemann [1983–])
WA	*Luthers Werke: Kritische Gesamtausgabe* [*Schriften*], 73 vols. (Weimar: H. Böhlau, 1883–2009)
WA Bi	*Luthers Werke: Kritische Gesamtausgabe: Bibel*, 12 vols. (Weimar: H. Böhlau, 1906–61), 7:206
WA Br	*Luthers Werke: Kritische Gesamtausgabe: Briefwechsel*, 18 vols. (Weimar: H. Böhlau, 1930–1985)
WA DB	*Luthers Werke: Kritische Gesamtausgabe: Deutsche Bibel*, 12 vols. (Weimar: H. Böhlau, 1906–61)
WA TR	*Luthers Werke: Kritische Gesamtausgabe: Tischreden*, 6 vols. (Weimar: H. Böhlau, 1912–21)

The Small Catechism

1529

TIMOTHY J. WENGERT

INTRODUCTION

The word *catechism* derives from the Greek verb *katēcheō*, "to sound over," and, hence, to teach by word of mouth.[a] In early Christianity, it simply stood for instructing, as in Gal. 6:6. From there it passed, transliterated, into ancient church Latin. By the fifth century, Augustine (354–430) was employing a Latin noun, *catechismus*, for basic instruction in church teaching. (The equivalent Greek noun also first appears around this time.) By the high or late Middle Ages, these basics came regularly to include especially the Ten Commandments, the Apostles' Creed, and the Lord's Prayer, to which sometimes the *Ave Maria* (Hail Mary) was added. Preachers were to give instruction in the catechism four times a year around the "Ember Weeks" (the third or fourth week in Advent; first week of Lent; Pentecost week; and around Holy

---

a   For the following history, see Robert Kolb, *Teaching God's Children His Teaching: A Guide for the Study of Luther's Catechism*, 2d ed. (St. Louis: Concordia Seminary Press, 2012); Charles P. Arand, *That I May Be His Own: An Overview of Luther's Catechisms* (St. Louis: Concordia, 2000); Timothy J. Wengert, *Martin Luther's Catechisms: Forming the Faith* (Minneapolis: Fortress Press, 2009); Albrecht Peters, *Commentary on Luther's Catechisms*, trans. Thomas H. Trapp, 5 vols. (St. Louis: Concordia, 2009–2013).

Cross Day [14 September], and penitents were to be quizzed in the confessional about their knowledge of the basics.

The Development of Luther's Small Catechism

This tradition is reflected in Luther's early preaching on the Ten Commandments, the Lord's Prayer, and the Creed,[b] and it continued into the 1520s and beyond. In 1520, Luther's sermons on these three parts were gathered into a single tract and in 1522 Luther expanded that into his prayer booklet.[c] Here, for the first time, Luther explains why he orders the parts of catechetical instruction the way he does.

A popular catechism by Dietrich Kolde (c. 1435–1515)[d] had used the Sacrament of Penance as its model for organizing these various parts—beginning with the Creed (which all in a state of sin could confess), moving to the Commandments and other lists of sins (as preparation for contrition and confession to a priest), before introducing the Lord's Prayer (as one prayer to be said to make satisfaction for the punishment for sin remaining after confession had removed one's guilt and reduced one's punishment from eternal to temporal). By contrast, already in 1522 Luther viewed the Commandments as the diagnosis of sin and need for grace, and thus placed them first in his catechetical writings. He then pointed to the Creed as grace, the medicine for sin, and finally he defined the Lord's Prayer as the plea to God to deliver the cure. His *Large Catechism* and *Small Catechism* would retain this same order for these same reasons.

In 1525, the first true forerunner to the *Small Catechism* appeared in Wittenberg from the presses of Nicholas Schirlentz and was quickly translated into *Niederdeutsch* (the dialect of the German lowlands from Magdeburg northward).[e] It contained

---

b   See, for example, *An Exposition of the Lord's Prayer for Simple Laymen* (1519), in LW 42:15–81.

c   See pp. 159–99 in this volume.

d   See Dietrich Kolde, *A Fruitful Mirror, or Small Handbook for Christians*, in Denis Janz, ed., *Three Reformation Catechisms: Catholic, Anabaptist, Lutheran* (Lewiston, NY: Edwin Mellen Press, 1982), 29–130.

e   Timothy J. Wengert, "Wittenberg's Earliest Catechism," *Lutheran Quarterly* 7 (1993): 247–60. For a translation into English, see the

the texts not only of the Ten Commandments, Creed, and Lord's Prayer, but also, for the first time, biblical texts for baptism and the Lord's Supper and instructions on prayers for morning, evening, and mealtimes. At nearly the same time, in his preface to the *German Mass* published in early 1526, Luther himself called on others to write catechisms, giving his *Little Prayer Book* as a guide and also suggesting another form for catechetical instruction.[f] This call resulted in a flood of catechisms produced in many areas by a variety of pastors and theologians.[g] In all, at least ten different booklets were produced in Wittenberg and elsewhere between 1525 and 1529.

Among the people who took up his charge was his former student Johann Agricola (1494–1566),[h] rector of the Latin School in Eisleben, who published three separate catechisms between 1527 and 1529. During the same period, Agricola and Philip Melanchthon (1497–1560) were locked in a struggle over the origin of true repentance, in which the former argued that it arose from the promise of the gospel and the latter from the preaching of the law. This diminution of the law was reflected in Agricola's catechisms, which placed the law as more or less an appendix and introduced it as equivalent to Cicero's rules for rhetoric.[i]

Johann Agricola's Lutheran catechetical instruction for young Christian children was published by Georg Rau in 1527, two years before the publication of Luther's *Small Catechism*. This first edition includes sections on the Ten Commandments, the Lord's Prayer, the Apostles' Creed, the Lord's Supper, and the Trinity.

   Booklet for Laity and Children, trans. Timothy J. Wengert, in Robert Kolb and James A. Nestingen, eds., *Sources and Contexts of the Book of Concord* (Minneapolis: Fortress Press, 2001), 1–12.

f   LW 53:64–67; TAL 3:142–46.

g   See Ferdinand Cohrs, ed., *Die evangelischen Katechismusversuche vor Luthers Enchiridion*, 4 vols. (Berlin: Hofmann, 1900–1902; reprint: Hildesheim: Ohms, 1978). For further discussion of the catechisms produced prior to 1529, see Timothy J. Wengert, *Law and Gospel: Philip Melanchthon's Debate with John Agricola of Eisleben over "Poenitentia"* (Grand Rapids: Baker, 1997), 47–75.

h   See also n. *m*, p. 206.

i   Wengert, *Law and Gospel*, 143.

Two other events triggered Luther's decision to write his own catechisms. First, in 1527, under pressure from Wittenberg and from parish pastors like Nicholas Hausmann (d. 1538) in Zwickau (who had also begged Luther to write a catechism), the elector of Saxony, John the Steadfast (1468–1532), decided to take the unprecedented step of authorizing an official visitation of the churches in his territories—something normally carried out by the local bishop. A team of four visitors, consisting of two representatives from the Saxon court and two from the university (one law professor [Jerome Schurff (1481–1554)] and one theologian [Melanchthon, elected by the theology faculty at Luther's insistence]), was sent out, beginning in the summer of 1527, with the tasks of evaluating the administrative, financial, practical, and theological conditions of the parishes, chapels, and monasteries. Luther himself participated in official visitation to parts of Saxony and Meissen from 22 October 1528 through 9 January 1529. As his preface to *the Small Catechism* made clear, these visits outside the confines of the university town of Wittenberg made him realize the abysmal level of Christian instruction, especially in the villages.

Second, in 1528 Johannes Bugenhagen (1485–1558), Wittenberg's chief pastor, was called away to help the cities of Braunschweig and Hamburg reform their churches. Luther was left with all the preaching duties and thus gave three sets of sermons on the catechism at the Vespers services in May, September, and December—still reflecting the medieval practice of expounding the catechism on the Embers.[j] These sermons, along with sermons on confession and the Lord's Supper from Holy Week, 1529, became the basis for the *Large Catechism*, first published in 1529.[k] At the same time, based in part upon summary sentences of the various parts of the Commandments, Creed, Lord's Prayer, and sacraments scattered throughout those sermons, Luther began writing very brief explanations designed to appear on individual broadsheets for each main part of the catechism

A portrait of Johannes Bugenhagen painted in 1532 by Lucas Cranach the Elder (1472–1553)

---

j   For an English translation of transcriptions of the third set of sermons, see LW 51:133–93.

k   See the *Large Catechism*, trans. James L. Schaaf, in BC, 377–480; TAL 2:278–415. For the Holy Week sermons, see *Martin Luther's Sermons from Holy Week and Easter, 1529*, trans. Irving Sandberg (St. Louis: Concordia, 1999).

and daily prayers and addressed to the *Hausvater* (the head of the household).

Although only one of these original Wittenberg printings has survived (a *Niederdeutsch* version of morning and evening prayer, reprints from other cities in both German dialects were gathered into booklet form and preserved. Luther completed work on the Ten Commandments, Creed, and Lord's Prayer in January 1529, when illness intervened, so that he did not complete work on the sacraments until the spring. Almost immediately, Nicholas Schirlentz published these broadsheets in booklet form, now with Luther's preface addressed to parish pastors and preachers, the household chart of Bible passages (later called the Table of Duties), and German liturgies for marriage and baptism (with Luther's prefaces), as well as biblical illustrations for each commandment, article of the Creed, petition of the Lord's Prayer, and sacrament. A second printing from 1531 included a new section on confession and an explanation of the words "Our Father in heaven."[1] The 1529 version was immediately translated into Latin (twice), and the 1531 version saw translations into many other European languages, including a paraphrastic version by Thomas Cranmer (1489–1556) into English.[/] For students learning biblical languages, several midcentury editions featured parallel texts in German, Latin, Greek, and Hebrew. All told, the six-

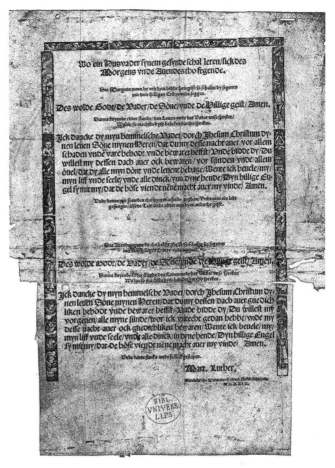

"Morning and Evening Prayers"
from the 1529 Wittenberg edition
of the *Small Catechsim* in the
Low German dialect

[/] The list in WA 30/1:782–804 includes Arabic, Czech, Danish, English, Estonian, Finnish, French, Icelandic, Italian, Slavonic, Latvian, Lithuanian, Dutch, Polish, Prussian (dialect), Swedish, Spanish, and Sorbian. For those printed in German-speaking lands, see also VD 16:L 5035–L 5177.

[1] Later editions published during Luther's lifetime in Wittenberg also occasionally included other additions. In 1536 Schirlentz added Scripture references under each picture along with texts of the *Te Deum* and *Magnificat* (LW 53:171–79). In 1543 he included the "Prayer against the Turks." The version from 1529 also included the *German Litany* (LW 53:153–70).

teenth century produced well over two hundred printings in various languages and dialects.

In contrast to one of Johann Agricola's catechisms, which boasted in its title to contain 130 questions,[m] Luther's *Small Catechism* used a single question throughout, *"Was ist das?"* ("What is this?"). This question invited simple paraphrase of the text in question rather than complicated explanation, thus implying that the catechism's texts were not obscure and needed simply to be put in other words for proper understanding. He added a second question for parts of the Lord's Prayer (for the first three petitions, "How does this come about?" and for the fourth, "What does [the word] daily bread mean?"). For the sacraments, four questions were used in addition to "What is this?"—questions asked about gifts and benefits and the role of faith and, for baptism, what using water signifies, and, for the Supper, the proper preparation.[2] The simple order for private confession contains a series of questions related to preparation for private confession to a pastor or priest.

2. Luther deemed only two texts obscure (the fourth petition and the water of baptism) and thus asked about the meaning of a word (daily bread) and about what an action (baptizing with water) signified.

Content

In contrast to Luther's reputation for verbosity, the *Small Catechism* was uniquely succinct. Using standard texts of medieval catechesis, Luther managed to explain these basics in terms consonant with major themes in his theology. Justification by faith alone had insisted that faith, demanded by the First Commandment, was the center of the Christian life. Thus, Luther took his explanation of that commandment ("fear, love, and trust in God") and applied it to the other nine commandments, where "fear and love" hearken back to the meaning of the First Commandment.[3] Justification also implied for Luther the proper distinction between law and gospel. His consistent use of *wir sollen* ("we are to"), found in both the commandments and his explanations, underscored what human beings *ought* to do but were not able to accomplish.[n]

3. He stated this explicitly in the *Large Catechism*, Ten Commandments, par. 326–29, in BC, 430.

---

m   Johann Agricola, *130 Common Questions for the Girl's School in Eisleben*, trans. Timothy J. Wengert, in Kolb and Nestingen, *Sources and Contexts*, 13–82.

n   See the *Large Catechism*, Ten Commandments, par. 316; Creed, par. 2; Lord's Prayer, par. 2, in BC, 428, 431, and 440–41, respectively.

First in explanations to the Creed, which Luther took as a description of God's triune actions of creating, redeeming, and making holy, Luther expounded the gospel of God's unmerited grace. God created "out of pure, fatherly, and divine goodness and mercy, without any merit or worthiness of mine at all"; God the Son ransomed humanity from the evil "kidnappers" of sin, death, and the devil by his suffering, death, and resurrection; God the Holy Spirit bestows faith and makes holy through forgiveness proclaimed in the Christian assembly.

The Lord's Prayer then pleads for God, now described as a loving Father, to fulfill the very promises made in the Creed by asking first for the word, faith in the word through the Holy Spirit (cf. the third article of the Creed), defeat of enemies of the word and faith (echoing the language of the second article), and then asking in thanksgiving for the gifts of creation (first article). Luther's explanations of petitions for forgiveness of sin, rescue from attacks on faith, and final deliverance from all evil underscore the centrality of God's mercy in the Christian's life. The "amen," which refers directly to commands and promises, also centers on the certainty of faith. Thus, the words "it is going to come about just like this" reflect the threefold paraphrase of the Creed's amen ("This is most certainly true"), which also appears in Luther's translation of Titus 3:5-8, used in question three of baptism, explaining the role of faith.

Luther's explanations of the sacraments move from what they are (question one, related to Christ's institution), to what effect and benefit they provide (forgiveness, life, and salvation), to the role of faith. The fourth question to each sacrament deals with the way they function in the believer's life: involving a daily drowning of the old creature and rising of the new in baptism (and, thus, in 1531 followed by an appended description of private confession, which moved from law to gospel) and the proper inward preparation of faith (as opposed to the outward, medieval practice of fasting) in the Supper.

This practical application continues in the prayers for morning, evening, and mealtimes and in "The Household Chart of Some Bible Passages." While affirming the common practice of regular prayers (based upon medieval models), Luther also directly criticized the late-medieval view of the monastic and mendicant life as being a higher form of Christianity.[4] Instead, in line with his view of Christian vocation in the world, he wrote

4. Such a chart echoed catechetical material prepared by the medieval theologian Jean Gerson (1363–1429).

this chart "for all kinds of holy orders and walks of life." He clearly rejected any division into more and less spiritual walks of life by including the responsibilities of ecclesiastical offices and governmental authority but primarily focusing on the "offices" of the German household of his day. This was also underscored by the inclusion of the liturgies of baptism and marriage, which constituted Christian households before God and in the world, and by the presence of woodcuts, which allowed even the unlettered in the household to visualize the catechism and its relation to Scripture.

The Purpose of the Small Catechism

With the *Small Catechism* in particular and other catechisms in the sixteenth century,[o] Lutheran catechists attempted to achieve several important goals. As a result of the visitations, Luther and others viewed many baptized members of congregations as woefully ignorant and in need of basic catechesis; their pastors were often ignorant themselves and inept teachers. A catechism provided a basic summary of the Christian faith. Moreover, catechisms continued to function as during the Middle Ages in the context of private confession while also providing basic liturgical texts to local pastors and congregants for marriage and baptism. In addition, catechisms provided, as it was often called, a "lay Bible," providing a summary of and introduction to the biblical message.[5] Thus, the combination of law (Commandments) and gospel (Creed and Lord's Prayer) and of word and sacraments gave people the tools by which to hear, understand, and even judge the preacher's sermon[6] and the basic sacramental actions in the congregation (baptism, confession, and the Lord's Supper), while also providing liturgies and biblical guidance for the home.

Even the booklet edition, despite its preface addressed to pastors and preachers, retained the *Small Catechism*'s focus on the household, adding woodcuts (as has been done in this transla-

5. This term was used already in the *Booklet for Laity and Children* of 1525, in the *Large Catechism*, and as a description of Luther's catechisms in the Epitome of the *Formula of Concord* (1576), in BC, 487, par. 5.

6. Mary Jane Haemig, "Laypeople as Overseers of the Faith: A Reformation Proposal," *Trinity Seminary Review* 27 (2006): 21–27.

o   See Johann Michael Reu, ed., *Quellen zur Geschichte des kirchlichen Unterrichts in der evangelischen Kirche Deutschlands zwischen 1530 und 1600*, 4 vols. in 9 (Gütersloh: Bertelsmann, 1904–1935; reprint: Hildesheim: Olms, 1976).

tion) and a chart of Bible passages for the household's various callings, while retaining the captions from each broadsheet addressed to householders. Indeed, in announcing his catechetical sermons to his Wittenberg congregation in November 1528, Luther encouraged the householders to send their children and servants to attend such preaching by stating, "You have been appointed their bishop and pastor; take heed that you do not neglect your office over them." In the first sermon given the next day he reiterated, "Every father of a family is a bishop in his house and the wife a bishopess. Therefore remember that you in your homes are to help us carry on the ministry as we do in the church."[p] With the publication of the *Small Catechism* in a booklet form that included Luther's preface to pastors and preachers, the *Catechism* took on a role in the Evangelical (Lutheran) congregations, thus carrying on the medieval practice of regular instruction in the basics of the Christian faith. Moreover, the *Catechism* quickly found its place in schools, especially with the translation into Latin already in 1529. Thus, households, congregations, and schools all played their part in catechesis.

Luther demonstrated in his explanations what he viewed as the proper way to interpret Scripture by recognizing the commands and promises. The woodcuts tied individual commandments to examples of their being broken in the Old Testament, articles of the Creed to God's biblical actions of creating, redeeming, and making holy, and the petitions of the Lord's Prayer to examples in the New Testament (with the exception of the first petition, which depicts preaching on the Sabbath from Exodus 20). The sacraments show contemporary celebrations in Wittenberg. Only in explaining the Sacrament of Baptism did Luther include several biblical texts (four in all), while in every other portion he simply concentrated on the specific catechetical text. However, in several instances, especially with the Creed, his paraphrases alluded to other biblical texts.

The explosion of catechetical writings in the sixteenth century demonstrates the deep commitment the reformers and their opponents had toward the education of the common people. Luther's *Small Catechism*, however, played an even more important part in catechesis as other preachers and teachers

---

p   See *Ten Sermons on the Catechism* (1528) in LW 51:136–37. These were delivered beginning on 29 November 1528.

7. Andreas Osiander (1498–1552).

began, almost immediately, to produce sermons and commentaries on Luther's work, beginning with the Nuremberg preacher Andreas Osiander's[7] *Children's Sermons* of the 1530s, itself a very popular publication throughout the sixteenth century.[q] To help students of theology learn their languages, there were even publications that provided, in four parallel columns, the text of the *Catechism* in German, Latin, Greek, and Hebrew. Moreover, it was not long before theologians were expanding Luther's small work with commentaries and biblically enriched outlines to theology, many of which were based upon or at least provided the text of Luther's *Catechism* as well.[r] Other catechisms, designed for students already proficient in the *Small Catechism*, were also published.[s] In some cases, this approach to instruction obscured the originality of Luther's own work, but it also preserved Luther's *Catechism* for later generations of Lutherans.

This translation uses WA 30/1:239–474, 537–819, and the *Bekenntnisschriften der evangelischen lutherischen Kirche*, 11th ed. (Göttingen: Vandenhoeck & Ruprecht, 1986), 499–542. It is based upon the translator's earlier work in *The Book of Concord*, ed. Robert Kolb and Timothy J. Wengert (Minneapolis: Fortress Press, 2000), 345–75, in which the *Marriage Booklet* and the *Baptismal Booklet* are revisions of Paul Zeller Strodach and Ulrich S. Leupold's translations in LW 53:106–115. The woodcut illustrations are from a facsimile edition of the Wittenberg printing of the *Catechism* from 1536. In that year, the printer Nicholas Schirlentz published a new edition of Luther's *Small Catechism*, in which, as in 1529, he again included woodcuts for each commandment, article of the Creed, petition of the Lord's

q   Mary Jane Haemig, "The Living Voice of the Catechism: German Lutheran Catechetical Preaching 1530–1580" (Harvard University: PhD dissertation, 1996).

r   For two examples among hundreds, see Heinrich Homel, *Catechismus D. Martini Lutheri Minor: Una cum perspicuis et dilucidis scholiis, ex Sacris Bibliis* (Wittenberg: Lehmann, 1584), with a preface by David Chytraeus; and Johann Tettelbach, *Das güldene Kleinodt: D. Martini Lutheri Catechismus, mit mehr christlichen Fragen erkleret* (n.p., 1571), with a preface by Tilemann Heshus.

s   For some of the earliest, see Reu, *Quellen*. Two of the most influential were Johannes Brenz, *Catechismus . . . Deutsch*, trans. Hartmann Beyer (Leipzig: Berwalt, 1553), and David Chytraeus, *Catechesis in Academia Rostochiana ex praelectionibus Davidis Chytraei collecta* (Wittenberg: Johann Krafft, 1554).

Prayer, sacrament, and the marriage and baptismal services, this time adding Bible references for the stories depicted. Such illustrations were included in almost all versions of Luther's catechisms published during his lifetime and beyond, and even in the 1584 official Latin translation of the *Book of Concord*.

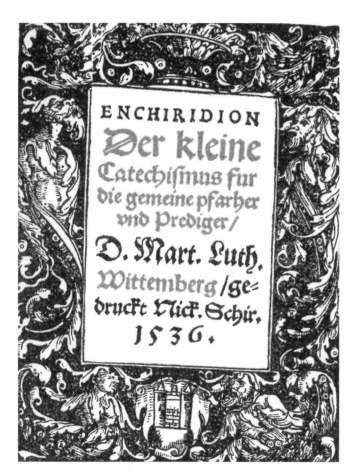

Cover of the 1536 printing of the *Small Catechism*.
Otto Albrecht, ed., *Der kleine Katechismus D. Martin Luthers nach der Ausgabe v. J. 1536* (Halle: Buchhandlung des Waisenhauses, 1905)

8. German (from the Latin and Greek): *Enchiridion*. In 1501, Erasmus of Rotterdam (1466–1536) had titled his instruction for the Christian life *Enchiridion militis Christiani* ("Handbook [or: Dagger] for the Christian Soldier").

9. This reflects both types of German clergy in Luther's day: pastors (*Pfarrherr*), who bore the major responsibility for pastoral care and worship in congregations, and preachers (*Prediger*).

10. The oldest surviving copy published in Wittenberg is from 1531.

11. See 1 Tim. 1:2 and 2 Tim. 1:2. Luther began using Pauline greetings for his letters exclusively, starting in 1522. When addressing specifically clergy, he sometimes used the greeting found in the Pastoral Epistles, as here.

12. In the medieval church, bishops were charged with regular visitation of their parishes, a formal examination of all aspects of parish life, often overseen by church officials sent by the diocese. In 1527, Elector John of Saxony (1468–1532) ordered an official visitation of churches in his lands, in the absence of cooperation from the local bishops, who normally provided such oversight. The teams consisted of two officials from the court, a professor of law (often Jerome Schurff) and a theologian (usually Philip Melanchthon, who was elected by the theology faculty). As something of an exception, Luther made official visitations of congregations in electoral Saxony and Meissen from October 22, 1528, through January 9, 1529, describing his experiences in a letter to Nicholas von Amsdorf (1483–1565) dated November

HANDBOOK[8]
THE SMALL CATECHISM
FOR ORDINARY PASTORS
AND PREACHERS[9]
MARTIN LUTHER
[1529][10]

[The Preface of Dr. Martin Luther]

MARTIN Luther,[t]

> To all faithful and upright pastors and preachers.
> Grace, mercy, and peace in Jesus Christ our Lord.[11]

The deplorable, wretched deprivation that I recently encountered while I was a visitor[12] has constrained and compelled[u] me to prepare this catechism, or Christian instruction,[v] in such a brief, plain, and simple version. Dear God have mercy, what misery I beheld! The ordinary person, especially in the villages, knows absolutely nothing about the Christian teaching, and unfortunately many pastors are completely unskilled and incompetent teachers. Yet supposedly they all bear the name Christian, are baptized, and receive the holy sacrament, even though they do not know the Lord's Prayer, the Creed, or the Ten Commandments![13] As a result they live like simple cattle or irrational pigs and, despite the fact that the gospel has returned, have masterfully learned how to misuse all their freedom. O you bishops! How are you ever going to answer to Christ, now that

---

t   This preface was printed in almost all booklet editions of the *Small Catechism*. In the 1531 edition, Luther's name begins with a large initial "M." Such decorative letters are also found at the beginning of the *Marriage Booklet*, the *Baptismal Booklet*, and, within the latter, for the first word of the exorcism and for the Gospel reading.

u   A German rhyme: *gezwungen und gedrungen*.

v   Similar to the introduction to the LC, Short Preface, par. 1-2 (BC, 383).

you have so shamefully neglected the people and have not exercised your office[14] for even a single second? May you escape punishment for this! You forbid the cup [to the laity in the Lord's Supper] and insist on observance of your human laws, while never even bothering to ask whether the people know the Lord's Prayer, the Creed, the Ten Commandments, or a single passage from God's Word. Woe to you forever![w]

Therefore, my dear sirs and brothers, whether pastors or preachers, for God's sake I beg that all of you would fervently take up your office, have pity on your people who are entrusted to you, and help us to bring the catechism to the people, especially to the young. In addition, I ask that those unable to do any better take up these charts and versions[15,x] and present them to the people word for word in the following manner:

In the first place, the preacher should above all take care to avoid changes or variations in the text and version of the Ten Commandments, the Lord's Prayer, the Creed, the sacraments, etc., but instead adopt a single version, stick with it, and always use the same one year after year. For the young and the unlettered people must be taught with a single, fixed text and version. Otherwise, if someone teaches one way now and another way next year—even when desiring to make improvements—the people become quite easily confused, and all the time and effort will go to waste.

The dear [church] fathers also understood this well. They used one form for the Lord's Prayer, the Creed, and the Ten Commandments.[16] Therefore, we, too, should teach these parts to the young and to people who cannot read in such a way that we neither change a single syllable nor present or recite it differently from one year to the next.[17] Therefore, choose for yourself whatever version you want and stick with it for good. To be sure, when you preach to educated and intelligent people, then you may demonstrate your erudition and discuss these parts with as much complexity and from as many different angles as you can. But with the young people, stick with a fixed, unchanging version and form. To begin with, teach them these parts: the Ten Commandments, the Creed, the Lord's Prayer, etc., following the

11, 1528 (LW 49:213-14). In 1528, Luther and Melanchthon together published under their coats of arms theological and practical instructions to the pastors. See LW 40:263-320 (where the title, incorrectly translated, should read *Instruction by the Visitors for the Parish Pastors of Electoral Saxony*).

13. In Luther's day the word *catechism* denoted these three parts, cited here in an order often found in late-medieval manuals.

14. For Luther, the "office" of church leaders constituted their duties and authority. He argued that pastors and bishops had primarily duties regarding teaching, preaching, and administration of the sacraments, in addition to their administrative responsibilities.

15. The word *table* (see n. *x* below) may refer especially to the original printing of the individual sections of the *Small Catechism* on separate broadsheets, which, like posters, could be displayed in homes, schools, and churches.

16. Luther is thinking here of the single Latin versions for the parts of the catechism used in the ancient and medieval church.

17. The reformers insisted that Christian catechesis was not just for the literate. Thus, they stressed memorization as a way of bringing "book learning" to all people. All levels of education stressed the importance of memorization—not as rote but as a way of keeping an author's message in the heart. Here, of course, Luther is not talking about his own explanations but the basic texts on which his explanations were based.

w   See Luther's criticism of the bishops in the *Instruction by the Visitors*, 1528 (LW 40:269-73).

x   Literally, in German: *tafeln und forme* (tables and forms).

text word for word, so that they can also repeat it back to you and learn it by heart.

Those who do not want to learn these things must be told how they deny Christ and are not Christians. They should also not be admitted to the sacrament, should not be sponsors for children at baptism, and should not exercise any aspect of Christian freedom,[y] but instead should simply be sent back home to the pope and his officials,[18] and, along with them, to the devil himself. Moreover, their parents and employers ought to deny them food and drink and advise them that the prince is disposed to drive such coarse people out of the country.

Although no one can or should force another person to believe,[z] nevertheless one should insist upon and hold the masses to this: that they know what is right and wrong among those with whom they wish to reside, eat and earn a living.[a] For example, if people want to live in a particular city, they ought to know and abide by the laws of the city whose protection they enjoy, no matter whether they believe or are at heart scoundrels and villains.

In the second place, once the people have learned the text well, then teach them to understand it, too, so that they know what it says. Take up again the form offered in these charts or some other short form that you may prefer, and adhere to it without changing a single syllable, just as was stated above regarding the text. Moreover, allow yourself ample time for it, because you need not take up all the parts at once but may instead handle them one at a time. After the people understand the First Commandment well, then take up the Second, and so on. Otherwise they will be so overwhelmed that they will hardly remember a single thing.

In the third place, after you have taught the people a short catechism like this one, then take up the large catechism[19] and impart to them a richer and fuller understanding. In this case, explain each individual commandment, petition, or part with its

18. German: *Officialen,* diocesan judges who decided administrative, disciplinary, and marriage cases.

19. Luther has in mind not only his own *Deutsch Katechismus,* which others came to call the *Large Catechism,* but also other catechetical books.

y   See also LC, Short Preface, par. 1-5 (BC, 383).

z   See the letter to Nicholas Hausmann dated March 17, 1522 (LW 48:399–402), the preface to *Instruction by the Visitors,* 1528 (LW 40:273), Luther's announcement for catechetical sermons in December 1528 (LW 51:136), and the LC, Lord's Supper, par. 42 (BC, 471).

a   See the letter to Thomas Löscher dated August 26, 1529 (LW 49:232–34), and LC, Short Preface, par. 2 (BC, 383).

various works, benefits and blessings, harm and danger, as you find treated at length in so many booklets. In particular, put the greatest stress on that commandment or part where your people experience the greatest need. For example, you must strongly emphasize the Seventh Commandment, which deals with stealing, with artisans and shopkeepers and even with farmers and household workers, because rampant among such people are all kinds of dishonesty and thievery.[b] Likewise, you must emphasize the Fourth Commandment to children and the common people, so that they are orderly, faithful, obedient, and peaceful.[c] Always adduce many examples from the Scriptures where God either punished or blessed such people.[20]

In particular, at this point[d] also urge governing authorities and parents to rule well and to send their children to school. Point out how they are obliged to do so and what a damnable sin they commit if they do not, for thereby, as the worst enemies of God and humanity, they overthrow and lay waste both the kingdom of God and the kingdom of the world.[21] Explain very clearly what kind of horrible damage they do when they do not help to train children as pastors, preachers, civil servants,[e] and the like, and tell them that God will punish them dreadfully for this. For in this day it is necessary to preach about these things, given that the extent to which parents and governing authorities are now sinning in these matters defies description. The devil, too, intends to do something horrible in all this.[f]

Finally,[22] because the tyranny of the pope has been abolished,[23] people no longer want to receive the sacrament, and they treat it with contempt. This, too, needs to be emphasized, with this caveat: That we should not compel anyone to believe or to receive the sacrament and should not fix any law or time

20. Luther's catechisms were always illustrated with woodcuts of biblical scenes. For the Fourth Commandment it was the drunkenness of Noah (Gen. 9:20-27); see illustration on p. 219.

21. As in the *Large Catechism* and his tracts on education listed below (nn. *d* and *f*), Luther emphasizes the importance of education for both church and government.

22. This introduces a final example of how to apply a specific topic from the catechism and is not a fourth step in catechesis. See LC, Lord's Supper, par. 39-84 (BC, 470-75).

23. Luther is referring to the strict medieval requirement to receive the Lord's Supper once a year, especially between Easter and Corpus Christi Day (eleven days after Pentecost).

---

b   See LC, Ten Commandments, par. 225-26 (BC, 416).

c   See LC, Ten Commandments, par. 105-66 (BC, 400-409).

d   This paragraph continues Luther's exposition of the Fourth Commandment. See LC, Ten Commandments, par. 167-78 (BC, 409-410); the *Treatise on Good Works*, 1520 (LW 44:85-100; TAL 1:257-367); and *A Sermon on Keeping Children in School*, 1530 (LW 46:207-58).

e   German: *schreiber*, literally, "notaries" or "clerks."

f   See the LC, Ten Commandments, par. 174-77 (BC, 410); *To the Councilmen of All Cities in Germany That They Establish and Maintain Christian Schools*, 1524 (LW 45:339-78; TAL 5, forthcoming); and *A Sermon on Keeping Children in School*, 1530 (LW 46:207-58).

24. In 1215 the Fourth Lateran Council, canon 21, stipulated that every Christian had to receive the Lord's Supper in the Easter season (up to Corpus Christi Day). See Luther's *Receiving Both Kinds in the Sacrament*, 1522 (LW 36:249), and *The Babylonian Captivity of the Church*, 1520 (LW 36:19–28; TAL 3:9–129).

25. For Luther, the Reformation reshaped the pastoral office, shifting it, for preachers, from moral exhortation to the proclamation of the gospel and, for pastors, from dispensing a grace effective "by the mere performance of rites" (*ex opere operato*) to the declaration of God's grace in audible and visible forms.

26. The titles for each section of the *Small Catechism* stem from the broadsheets of 1529 and were retained in subsequent booklet editions. (The Latin translation of 1529 addresses schoolteachers and students.) In 1531, this sentence was placed on a separate title page, which depicted the Lamb of God above and Luther's coat of arms (the "Luther rose") below. In the booklet form, Luther followed his ordering discussed in the *Little Prayer Book*, moving from Commandments (which diagnose human sin), to the Creed (which describes God's grace), to the Lord's Prayer (which begs God for the very grace needed to fulfill the Commandments). This differed from many medieval catechisms that were oriented toward the Sacrament of

or place for it. Instead, we should preach in such a way that the people make themselves come without our law and just plain compel[g] us pastors to administer the sacrament to them. This can be done by telling them: One has to worry that whoever does not desire or receive the sacrament at the very least once or four times a year despises the sacrament and is no Christian, just as anyone who does not listen to or believe the gospel is no Christian. For Christ did not say, "Omit this," or "Despise this," but instead [1 Cor. 11:25], "Do this, as often as you drink it. . . ." He really wants it to be done and not completely omitted or despised. "DO this," he says.

Those[h] who do not hold the sacrament in high esteem indicate that they have no sin, no flesh, no devil, no world, no death, no dangers, no hell. That is, they believe they have none of these things, although they are up to their neck in them and belong to the devil twice over. On the other hand, they indicate that they need no grace, no life, no paradise, no heaven, no Christ, no God, nor any other good thing. For if they believed that they had so much evil and needed so much good, they would not neglect the sacrament, in which help against such evil is provided and in which so much good is given. It would not be necessary to compel them with any law to receive the sacrament. Instead, they would come on their own, rushing and running to it; they would compel themselves to come and would insist that you give them the sacrament.

For these reasons, you do not have to make any law concerning this, as the pope did.[24] Only emphasize clearly the benefit and the harm, the need and the blessing, the danger and the salvation in this sacrament. Then they will doubtless come on their own without your forcing them. If they do not come, give up on them and tell them that those who pay no attention to nor feel their great need and God's gracious help belong to the devil. However, if you either do not stress this or make it into a law or poison, then it is your fault if they despise the sacrament. How can they help but neglect it, if you sleep and remain silent? Therefore, pastors and preachers, take note! Our office has now become a completely different thing than it was under

g   German: *dringen, und . . . zwingen*, a rhymed couplet. The Lord's Supper was celebrated each Sunday at St. Mary's Church in Wittenberg, although not many received it that often.

h   The German text uses the third person singular.

the pope.[25] It has now become serious and salutary. Thus, it now involves much toil and work, many dangers and attacks[i] and, in addition, little reward or gratitude in the world. But Christ himself will be our reward, so long as we labor faithfully. May the Father of all grace grant it, to whom be praise and thanks in eternity through Christ, our Lord. Amen.

The Ten Commandments: In a Simple Way in Which the Head of a House Is to Present[j] Them to the Household[26]

Worship of the golden calf (Exodus 32)[27]

The First [Commandment][k]

You are to[l] have no other gods.[28]
What is this?[29] Answer:
We are to fear, love, and trust God above all things.

---

i   German: *Anfechtung.*

j   German: *furhalten,* used for each section of the catechism, except for the prayers, where Luther suggests they be "taught" (i.e., memorized).

k   This word, lacking in the editions of 1529–1535, is present in all other editions of the *Small Catechism* and in the *Book of Concord* of 1580.

Penance and thus began with the Creed, which a person in a state of sin could admit was true, moved to the Ten Commandments as one of many lists of sins the penitent was required to confess, and finally to the Lord's Prayer, often without explanation, as one prayer necessary to recite to satisfy one's remaining temporal punishment for sin.

27. In the printings of the *Small Catechism* during Luther's lifetime, each commandment, article of the Creed, petition of the Lord's Prayer, and sacrament was accompanied by a woodcut and (from 1536) references to the Bible story on which each picture was based. Woodcuts similar to those used in the *Small Catechism* were also included in the *Large Catechism* (see WA 30/1:133–210).

28. Luther uses a common form of the Decalogue that does not always correspond to the texts of either Exodus 20 or Deuteronomy 5 in the Luther Bible. As a result, some later editions, including the Nuremberg editions of 1531 and 1558, correct the text here and elsewhere according to the biblical text. The italicized portions throughout the *Small Catechism* were originally printed using larger type.

29. German: *Was ist das?* This question indicates that Luther viewed his responses more as paraphrase than as a disclosure of hidden meaning. The sense is "In other words" or "That is to say."

Blasphemy of Shelomith's son
(Lev. 24:10-16)

Breaking the Sabbath (Num. 15:32-36)

30. Luther uses these two verbs to refer back to the First Commandment. See *Instruction by the Visitors*, 1528 (LW 40:276–77) and LC, Ten Commandments, par. 321–27 (BC, 429–30).

The Second [Commandment]

You are not to take the name of your God in vain.[m]
What is this? Answer:
We are to fear and love[30] God, so that[n] we do not curse, swear,[o] practice magic, lie, or deceive using God's name, but instead use that very name in every time of need to call on, pray to, praise, and give thanks to God.

The Third [Commandment]

You are to hallow the day of rest.[p]
What is this? Answer:
We are to fear and love God, so that we do not despise preaching or God's Word, but instead keep that Word holy and gladly hear and learn it.

l Throughout the Commandments the German word *sollen* is translated "are to," as a way of avoiding the confusion in English, where "shall" can mean either "ought to" or "will," and to clarify the paraphrastic nature of Luther's explanations.

m Following the editions of 1529–1535. The Nuremberg editions of 1531 and 1558 add "for the Lord will not hold that one guiltless who takes his name in vain."

n German: *das.* This may be rendered either modally ("by not doing") or consequentially ("with the result that we do not").

o German: *schweren,* here used in the sense of false oaths. See the LC, Ten Commandments, par. 65–66 (BC, 394–95).

p German: *Feiertag,* literally, "day of rest" (like the Hebrew word *sabbath*), but generally for Sunday and other "holy days." This (traditional) rendering differed from Luther's translation of the text in Exodus 20 and Deuteronomy 5, where he used the terms "holy day" and "Sabbath."

The Fourth [Commandment]

You are to honor your father and your mother.
What is this? Answer:
We are to fear and love God, so that we neither despise nor anger our parents and others in authority[q] but instead honor, serve, obey, love, and respect.

The drunkenness of Noah
(Gen. 9:20–27)

The Fifth [Commandment]

You are not to kill.
What is this? Answer:
We are to fear and love God, so that we neither endanger nor harm the lives of our neighbors,[r] but instead help and support them in all of life's needs.

Cain slays Abel (Gen. 4:1–16)

---

q   German: *Herrn*, literally, "lords," but used here to denote those in authority, e.g., *Landesherrn* (princes), *Hausherr* (head of the house), or *Pfarrherr* (pastors).

r   Here and in the following explanations, the word *neighbor* is singular in the German.

David and Bathsheba (2 Samuel 11)

The theft by Achan (Joshua 7)

The Sixth [Commandment]

You are not to commit adultery.

What is this? Answer:

We are to fear and love God, so that we lead pure and decent lives in word and deed and each person loves and honors his [or her] spouse.

The Seventh [Commandment]

You are not to steal.

What is this? Answer:

We are to fear and love God, so that we neither take our neighbors' money or property nor acquire them by using shoddy merchandise or crooked deals, but instead help them to improve and protect their property and income.

The Eighth [Commandment]

You are not to bear false witness against your neighbor.

What is this? Answer:

We are to fear and love God, so that we do not tell lies about our neighbors, betray or slander them, or destroy their reputations. Instead we are to come to their defense, speak well of them, and interpret everything they do in the best possible light.

In Latin and Greek versions of Daniel, this story of Susanna and her false accusers was added and is part of the Apocrypha.

The Ninth [Commandment]

You are not to covet your neighbor's house.

What is this? Answer:

We are to fear and love God, so that we do not try to trick our neighbors out of their inheritance or property or try to get it for ourselves by claiming to have a legal right to it and the like, but instead be of help and service to them in keeping what is theirs.

Jacob cheating Laban
(Gen. 30:25–43)

Joseph and Potiphar's
wife (Genesis 39)

The Tenth [Commandment]

You are not to covet your neighbor's wife, male or female servant, cattle or whatever is his.

What is this? Answer:

We are to fear and love God, so that we do not entice, force, or steal away from our neighbors their spouses,[s] household workers, or livestock, but instead urge them to stay and fulfill their obligations.

What then does God say about all these commandments? Answer: God says the following: "*I, the LORD your God, am a jealous God. Against those who hate me I visit the sin of the fathers on the children up to the third and fourth generation. But I do good to those who love me and keep my commandments to the thousandth generation.*"[t]

What is this? Answer:

God threatens to punish all who break these commandments. Therefore we are to fear his wrath and do nothing contrary to these commandments. However, he promises grace and every good thing to all those who keep these commandments. Therefore we also are to love and trust him and gladly act according to his commands.

---

s   German: *sein weib* (his wife). In sixteenth-century German, *Weib* was the common word for *Frau*.

t   This text does not follow Exod. 20:5-6 or Deut. 5:9-10 as translated in the Luther Bible.

The Creed: In the Very Simple Way in Which the Head of a House Is to Present It to the Household[31]

The First Article: On Creation

I believe in God, the Father almighty, CREATOR[u] of heaven and earth.

What is this? Answer:

I believe that God has created me together with all that exists.[v] God has given me and still preserves my body and soul: eyes, ears and all my abilities; reason and all mental faculties.[32] In addition, God daily and abundantly provides shoes and clothing, food and drink, house and farm, spouse[w] and children, fields, livestock and all property—along with all the necessities and nourishment for this body and life.[x] God protects me against all danger and shields and preserves me from all evil. And all this is done out of pure, fatherly, and divine goodness and mercy, without any merit or worthiness of mine at all! For all of this I owe[y] it to God to thank and praise, serve and obey him. This is most certainly true.[33]

God depicted as a bearded man giving a blessing, surrounded by animals and encircled by clouds and the four winds (cf. Gen. 1–2).

31. Traditionally, the Creed was divided into twelve articles (for the twelve apostles). Luther here, as already in the *Little Prayer Book*, returns to a still older tradition of dividing the Creed into three parts for the Trinity.

32. Luther here explains more fully what he means by body, using *gelieder* (abilities) to sum up the bodily functions and *sinne* (mental faculties) to sum up the soul's functions.

33. Luther's paraphrase of "Amen." See the explanation to "Amen" in the Lord's Prayer, p. 230, and the reference to the third question in Holy Baptism, p. 231, where the phrase is used to translate Titus 3:8.

---

u   Capitalized in the original.

v   German: *Creaturen*.

w   German: *weib*, literally, wife.

x   Some modern commentators and translators connect "shoes . . . property" to the preceding sentence. However, the Latin translations of 1529, the capitalization of "In addition" (*Dazu*) in the original text, and the placement of verbs at the end of each sentence throughout this explanation argue for its inclusion with what follows.

y   German: *schüldig* (indebted).

Christ crucified
(Matthew 26–27)

34. Throughout this explanation, Luther uses the familiar image of a lord's responsibility to rescue any kidnapped or imprisoned subjects. See also LC, Creed, par. 27–31 (BC, 434–45).

The Second Article: On Redemption

And[z] [I believe] in Jesus Christ, his only Son, our LORD, *who was conceived by the Holy Spirit, born of the Virgin Mary, suffered under Pontius Pilate, was crucified, died, and was buried. He descended into hell, on the third day he rose, ascended into heaven, is seated at the right hand of God, the almighty Father, from where he will come to judge the living and the dead.*

What is this? Answer:

I believe that Jesus Christ, true God, born of the Father in eternity, and also a true human being, born of the Virgin Mary, is my LORD.[34] He has redeemed me, a lost and condemned human being. He has purchased and freed me from all sins, from death, and from the power of the devil, not with gold or silver but with his holy, precious blood and with his innocent[a] suffering and death. He has done all this in order that I may belong to him, live under him in his kingdom, and serve him in eternal righteousness, innocence,[b] and blessedness, just as he is risen from the dead and lives and rules eternally. This is most certainly true.

---

z   The text corresponds to that used in the 1529 version.

a   German: *Unschüldigen*, literally, "not owed" or "not guilty."

b   German: *Unschuld*, literally, "something not owed."

The Third Article: On Being Made Holy[35]

I believe in the Holy Spirit, one holy Christian church,[36] the community of the saints,[c] forgiveness of sins, resurrection of the flesh and an eternal life. AMEN.

What is this? Answer:

I believe that by my own reason or powers[37] I cannot believe in Jesus Christ my Lord or come to him. But instead the Holy Spirit has called me through the gospel, enlightened me with his gifts, made me holy and kept me in the true faith, just as he calls, gathers, enlightens, and makes holy the whole Christian church[d] on earth and keeps it with Jesus Christ in the one common, true faith. Daily in this Christian church the Holy Spirit abundantly forgives all sins—mine and those of all believers. On the last day the Holy Spirit will raise me and all the dead and will give to me and all believers in Christ eternal life. This is most certainly true.

The first Pentecost with tongues of fire coming from the disciples' mouths (cf. Acts 2 and Rev. 11:5)

The Lord's Prayer: In the Very Simple Way in Which the Head of a House Is to Present It to the Household

Our Father, you who are in heaven.[e]

[38][What is this? Answer:

With these words God wants to attract us, so that we come to believe he is truly our Father and we are truly his children, in order that we may ask[f] him boldly and with complete confidence, just as loving children ask their loving father.][39]

35. The English word *sanctification* does not preserve the linguistic connection between the Holy Spirit and the Holy Spirit's activity. See LC, Creed, par. 35–36 (BC, 435–36). The sharp distinction between "justification" and "sanctification" first arises later in the sixteenth century.

36. German translations of the Creed before and after the Reformation translate *ecclesia catholica* as Christian church.

37. German: *vernunfft noch krafft.* Luther here is attacking the late-medieval notion that a person could come to faith through his or her own capacities of will (power [Latin: *virtus*]) or intellect (reason [Latin: *ratio*]).

38. Luther first added this explanation to the introduction in the edition of 1531.

39. This explanation, although added later, epitomized Luther's approach to prayer: *not* as a mere recitation of

---

c   German: *heiligen,* literally, holy ones.

d   German: *die gantze Christenheit.* German versions of the Creed predating Luther use this phrase to translate the Latin *ecclesia catholica.*

e   The text of the Lord's Prayer follows a common form used in Wittenberg and not the version in the Luther Bible.

f   German: *bitten,* which means both "ask" and "pray" in early New High German.

Preaching the Word of God
(Exod. 20:8-11, 19)

The First Request[g]

May your name be hallowed.[h]

What is this? Answer:

To be sure, God's name is holy in itself, but we ask in this prayer that it may also become holy in and among[i] us.

How does this come about?[j] Answer:

Whenever the Word of God is taught clearly and purely and we live according to it in a holy manner, as God's children. To this end help us, dear Father in heaven![40] However, whoever teaches and lives otherwise than the Word of God teaches profanes the name of God among us. Preserve us from this, heavenly Father!

words but as an earnest begging God for help. In Luther's German the word "prayer" (*beten*) was always associated with asking, so that praise and thanksgiving, as in the explanation to the Second Commandment, were viewed separately.

40. Here Luther combines the "Our Father" with the first petition in an actual paraphrase. Throughout his explanations, he refers to God as Father.

41. See above, the explanation to the third article of the Apostles' Creed.

42. Here Luther connects the third petition's fulfillment to the first two petitions, first quoting the text of those requests and then the meaning (Word and faith).

g   German: *Bitte*, traditionally translated "petition."

h   German: *Geheiliget*, literally, "made holy" or "sanctified."

i   German: *bey*.

j   German: *geschicht*, the same verb as in the third petition.

The Second Request

May your kingdom come.

What is this? Answer:

In fact, God's kingdom comes on its own without our prayer, but we ask in this prayer that it may also come to us.

How does this come about? Answer:

Whenever our heavenly Father gives us his Holy Spirit, so that through his grace we believe his Holy Word and live godly lives here in time and hereafter in eternity.[41]

Because Luther interpreted the Second Petition as a plea for the Holy Spirit, the picture is the same as for the Third Article. See above, p. 225.

The Third Request

May your will come about on earth as in heaven.

What is this? Answer:

In fact, God's good and gracious will comes about without our prayer, but we ask in this prayer, that it may also come about in and among[k] us.

How does this come about? Answer:

Whenever God breaks and hinders every evil scheme and will—as are present in the will of the devil, the world, and our flesh[l]—that would not allow us to hallow God's name and would prevent the coming of his kingdom, and instead whenever God strengthens us and keeps us firm in his Word and in faith until the end of our lives.[42] This is his gracious and good will.

Christ bearing the cross
(Matt. 27:31-32)

k   German: *bey.*

l   The syntax of this sentence is rather awkward in the German. Note similarities to the second article of the Creed.

Jesus feeding the five thousand
(John 6:1-15)

The Fourth Request

Give us today our daily bread.

What is this? Answer:

In fact, God gives daily bread without our prayer even to all evil people, but we ask in this prayer that God cause us to recognize what our daily bread is and to receive it with thanksgiving.

What then does [the phrase] "daily bread" mean? Answer:

Everything included in the necessities and nourishment for our bodies,[43] such as food, drink, clothing, shoes, house, farm,[m] fields, livestock, money, property, an upright[44] spouse, upright children, upright members of the household,[45] upright and faithful rulers, good government, good weather, peace, health, decency, honor, good friends, faithful neighbors, and the like.

43. See the explanation to the first article of the Apostles' Creed above.

44. German: *frum.* In the sixteenth century this word meant "upright, honest, competent, capable, well-behaved, sensible," but not so much, as in modern usage, "pious or godly."

45. German: *Gesinde*, the house servants and workers. In Luther's day the household was the center of economic activity and thus included both family members and laborers.

46. German: *angefochten*, the verbal form of *Anfechtung*, an important descriptor for Luther of the Christian life. See the Preface to the *Small Catechism*, above, p. 212, and his *Preface to the Wittenberg Edition of Luther's German Writings*, 1539 (LW 34:286–87; this volume, pp. 475–87).

m   German: *hoff* (farm buildings or farmstead).

The Fifth Request

And remit our debts," as we remit what our debtors owe.
What is this? Answer:

We ask in this prayer that our heavenly Father would not regard our sins nor deny these requests on their account, for we are worthy of nothing for which we ask, nor have we earned it. Instead we ask that God would give us all things by grace, for we daily sin much and indeed deserve only punishment. So, on the other hand, we, too, truly want heartily to forgive and gladly to do good to those who sin against us.

Parable of the Unforgiving
Servant (Matt. 18:23-35)

The Sixth Request

And lead us not in temptation.
What is this? Answer:

It is true that God tempts no one, but we ask in this prayer that God would preserve and keep us, so that the devil, the world, and our flesh may not deceive us or mislead us into false belief, despair, and other great shame and vice, and that, although we may be attacked[46] by them, we may finally prevail and gain the victory.

The temptation of Christ
(Matt. 4:1-11). Note Jesus with
sheep and the devil with a wolf.

n German: *Schulde.*

Jesus and the Syrophoenician
woman (Matt. 15:21–28)

47. Some later editions of the *Catechism*,
printed after Luther's death, add the
doxology ("For the kingdom, the power
and the glory are yours, now and
forever"). Although found in Erasmus's
editions of the Greek New Testament
and in Luther's translation into
German, Luther himself consistently
followed the medieval usage in
catechesis and omitted it.

48. For the command to pray and the
promise to hear prayers, see LC, Lord's
Prayer, par. 4–21 (BC, 441–43).

The Seventh Request

But deliver us from evil.

What is this? Answer:

We ask in this prayer, as in the summation, that our Father in heaven may deliver us from all kinds of evil—affecting body or soul, property or reputation—and at last, when our final hour comes, may grant us a blessed end and take us by grace from this valley of tears to himself in heaven.

Amen.[47]

What is this? Answer:

That I should be certain that such petitions are acceptable to and heard by our Father in heaven, for he himself commanded us to pray like this and has promised to hear us.[48] "Amen, amen" means "Yes, yes, it should come about just like this."

Holy Baptism (Matt. 28:16-20)
as practiced in Wittenberg

The Sacrament of Holy Baptism:
In a Simple Way in Which the Head of a House
Is to Present It to the Household[49]

First

What is Baptism? Answer:

Baptism is not simply plain water. Instead it is water enclosed in God's command[50] and connected with God's Word.

What then is this Word of God? Answer:

Where our LORD Christ says in Matt. 28[:19], "Go into all the world, teach all nations,[o] and baptize them in the name of the Father and of the Son and of the Holy Spirit."

Second

What gifts or benefits does Baptism grant?[51] Answer:

It brings about forgiveness of sins, redeems from death and the devil, and gives eternal salvation to all who believe it, as the words and promise of God declare.

What are these words and promise of God? Answer:

Where our LORD Christ says in Mark 16[:16], "Whoever believes and is baptized will be saved, but whoever does not believe will be damned."

Third

How can water do such great things? Answer:

Clearly the water does not do it, but the Word of God, which is with and alongside[p] the water, and faith, which trusts this Word of God in the water. For without the Word of God the water is plain water and not a baptism, but with the Word of God it is a baptism, that is, a grace-filled water of life and a "bath of the new birth in the Holy Spirit," as St. Paul says to Titus in chapter 3[:5-8], *"through the bath of rebirth and renewal of the Holy Spirit, which he*

49. Baptism, often missing from medieval catechesis (because adults were thought to have sinned away the grace associated with that sacrament), was central to Luther's understanding of the Christian life of faith, as the answer to the fourth question made clear.

50. Luther here moves from the command to baptize to the promises contained in baptism and to faith in such promises.

51. Luther moves from the definition of baptism to its effects.

---

o   German: *Heiden* (heathen).

p   German: *mit und bey.*

52. In Luther's day, baptisms were often performed by immersing the infant in the water and drawing it out again. Luther preferred this method. See *The Babylonian Captivity of the Church*, 1520 (LW 36:67–68; TAL 3:9–129).

53. Literally, the Old Adam.

54. In 1531 paragraphs 15–29 replaced the earlier *A Short Order of Confession*, 1529 (LW 53:116–18), which was found in one Latin version of the *Small Catechism* from 1529 in this place and in one German version of the *Small Catechism* from 1529 following the *Baptismal Booklet*. In 1532 Luther defended this addition and the use of private confession among evangelicals in a letter to the town council and congregation in Frankfurt on the Main, "An Open Letter to Those in Frankfurt on the Main, 1533," trans. John D. Vieker, *Concordia Journal* 16 (1990): 333–51 (= WA 30/3:565–71). In 1531, this title was placed in the same illustrations used for the title page of the *Small Catechism*. Luther, in contrast to medieval theology, viewed confession and forgiveness as the regular living out of baptism's significance, as discussed in question four on baptism.

55. See LC, "A Brief Exhortation to Confession" (BC, 476–80), especially par. 15 (BC, 478). Already in some of his earliest writings from 1517 and later, Luther distinguished two parts of penitence—sorrow for sin (confession) and absolution (forgiveness). This he contrasted to the medieval, Scholastic definition of the Sacrament of Penance as consisting of contrition, confession,

richly poured out over us through Jesus Christ our Savior, so that through that very grace we may be justified[q] *heirs in hope of eternal life. This is*[r] *most certainly true."*

Fourth

What then does such baptism with water signify?[52] Answer:

It signifies that the old creature[53] in us with all sins and evil desires is to be drowned and die through daily contrition and repentance and, on the other hand, that daily a new person is to come forth and rise up to live before God in righteousness and purity forever.

Where is this written? Answer:

St. Paul says in Rom. 6[:4] "We were buried with Christ through baptism in death, so that, just as Christ was raised from the dead through the glory of the Father, we, too, are to walk in a new life."

How Simple People Are to Be Taught to Confess[54]

What is confession? Answer:

Confession consists of two parts.[55] One is that we confess our sins. The other is that we receive the absolution, that is, forgiveness, from the confessor as from God himself and by no means doubt but firmly believe that our sins are thereby forgiven before God in heaven.

Which sins is a person to confess?

Before God one is to acknowledge the guilt for all sins, even those of which we are not aware, as we do in the Lord's Prayer.[56]

However, before the confessor we are to confess only those sins of which we have knowledge and which trouble us.[57]

Which sins are these?

q   Versions from 1536 and thereafter read instead "righteous and," which is parallel to Luther's Bible.

r   Versions from 1536 and thereafter insert "Surely."

Here, in light of the Ten Commandments, reflect on your place in life:[s] whether you are father, mother, son, daughter, master, mistress, servant;[58] whether you have been disobedient, unfaithful, lazy, ill-tempered, unruly, or quarrelsome;[t] whether you have harmed anyone by word or deed; whether you have stolen, neglected, wasted, or injured anything.

Please provide me with a brief form of confession! Answer:[59]
You are to say to the confessor:[60]
"Honorable, dear sir, I ask you[u] to listen to my confession and declare to me forgiveness for God's sake."

Then say this:
"I, a poor sinner, confess before God that I am guilty of all [my] sins.[61] In particular, I confess in your presence that I am a manservant, maidservant, etc., but I unfortunately serve my master[v] unfaithfully, for in this and that instance I did not do what they told me; I made them angry and caused them to curse; I neglected to do my duty and allowed harm to occur.

"I have also spoken and acted impudently. I have quarreled with my equals; I have grumbled about and sworn at my mistresses, etc. I am sorry for all this and ask for grace. I want to do better."

A master or mistress may say the following:
"In particular I confess to you that I have not faithfully cared for my child, the members of my household or my spouse[w] to the glory of God. I have cursed, set a bad example with indecent words and deeds, done harm to my neighbors,[x] spoken evil of them, overcharged them, and sold them inferior goods and short-changed them," and whatever else he [or she] has done against the commands of God and their walk of life, etc.

---

s German: *Stand* (station or walk of life).
t The Wittenberg editions of 1535 and following omit: "ill-tempered, unruly, or quarrelsome."
u Here and throughout Luther uses the formal form of address.
v Luther shifts from the singular (master) to the plural (they).
w German: *weib* (wife).
x German: singular.

and satisfaction, where "satisfaction" meant doing good works that satisfied the remaining *temporal* punishment for sin, the eternal punishment having been removed in the priest's absolution.

56. See the fifth petition.

57. This contrasts to the medieval practice, which required that the penitent confess all mortal sins committed since the last confession. See below.

58. The basic positions in a sixteenth-century German household.

59. Much of this form builds upon the medieval practice of private confession.

60. The Wittenberg church still practiced private confession to a pastor, as is depicted on the altarpiece from 1547 painted by Lukas Cranach (1472–1553), which showed the chief pastor in Wittenberg, Johannes Bugenhagen, holding the "keys," forgiving one confessant and binding the sins of another. In an emergency, Luther taught that anyone could function in this way for a Christian whose conscience was especially oppressed by sin.

61. This is the general confession referred to below in par. 25. It prefaces the particular confession here and is the implied beginning of the confessions in paragraphs 23 and 24. In other cases the "general confession" refers to public confession, that is, words spoken at the conclusion of the sermon in worship. Cf. SA, pt. III, art. iii, par. 13 (BC, 314).

62. See *A Discussion on How Confession Should Be Made*, 1520 (LW 39:27–47) and CA XXV.7–12 (BC, 72–75). Medieval practice insisted that the penitent confess *all* sins to the priest with the threat that any omissions placed the entire confession in jeopardy. As a result, long lists of possible sins were often a part of medieval prayer books and catechisms. Contrary to this, the Wittenberg reformers insisted that no such rule should be enforced but, rather, that the individual conscience should be respected and encouraged to seek absolution for particularly those sins that oppressed them.

63. See above, n. 61, p. 233. Luther could have in mind expanding this with the words of the fuller version of general public confession spoken after the sermon by the preacher.

64. German: *angefochten*. See above, n. 46, p. 228.

If, however, some individuals[y] do not find themselves burdened by these or greater sins, they are not to worry or search for and invent further sins and thereby turn confession into torture.[62] Instead mention one or two that you are aware of, as follows: "In particular I confess that I cursed once, likewise that one time I was inconsiderate in my speech, one time I neglected this or that, etc." Let that suffice.

If you are aware of no sins at all (which is really quite unlikely), then do not mention any in particular, but instead receive forgiveness on the basis of the general confession,[63] which you make to God in the presence of the confessor.

Thereupon the confessor is to say:
"God be gracious to you and strengthen your faith. AMEN."

Then let [the confessor] say:
"Do you also believe that my forgiveness is God's forgiveness?"
[Answer:] "Yes, dear sir."

Thereupon he may say:
"'Let it be done for you according to your faith.'[z] And I by the command of our LORD Jesus Christ[a] forgive you your sin in the name of the Father and of the Son and of the Holy Spirit. Amen. Go in peace."[b]

A confessor, by using additional passages of Scripture, can in fact comfort and encourage to faith those whose consciences are heavily burdened or who are distressed and under attack.[64] This is only to be an ordinary form of confession for simple people.

---

y   German: singular.
z   Matt. 8:13.
a   Matt. 16:19; 18:18; John 20:23.
b   Mark 5:34; Luke 7:50; 8:48.

The Sacrament of the Altar:
In a Simple Way in Which the Head of a House Is to Present It to the Household[65]

The distribution of the Lord's Supper (Matt. 26:26-28).
Above the altar is a depiction of the Last Supper
with Christ communing with Judas.[66] A pastor wearing
a chasuble offers the bread to a kneeling man and
an assistant the cup to a kneeling woman. On either side
of the altar others are waiting to receive the elements.

What is the Sacrament of the Altar?[67] Answer:

It is the true body and blood of our Lord Jesus Christ under the bread and wine, instituted by Christ himself for us Christians to eat and to drink.

Where is this written? Answer:

The holy evangelists, Matthew, Mark, and Luke, and St. Paul write thus:

"Our LORD Jesus Christ, on the night in which he was betrayed, took the bread, gave thanks and broke it and gave it to his disciples and said, 'Take; eat; this is my body which is given for you. Do this in remembrance of me.'

65. Medieval catechesis was often viewed as preparing persons for the Sacrament of Penance and, hence, did not emphasize the Lord's Supper. Here Luther insisted on the twin gifts of Christ's presence and forgiveness in the Supper, which are received by faith. He thus spelled out a view of the Sacrament of the Altar that differed from those of Ulrich Zwingli (1484–1531), who denied Christ's real presence in the meal, and of Wittenberg's Roman opponents, who argued that the Supper was an unbloodied sacrifice to God offered by the priests on behalf of the sins of the congregation or those for whom the celebration had been purchased, in which faith was unnecessary for the sacrament's effectiveness.

66. This underscored the Lutheran insistence, over against Ulrich Zwingli and others, that unbelievers also received Christ's body and blood in the Supper.

67. The first three questions here match those in the section on baptism: what is it; what are its benefits; and who receives it properly (namely, through faith)?

"In the same way he also took the cup after the supper, gave thanks and gave it to them and said, 'Take, and drink from it, all of you. This cup is the New Testament in my blood, which is shed for you for the forgiveness of sins. Do this, as often as you drink it, in remembrance of me.'" [c]

What is the benefit of such eating and drinking? Answer:
The words, *"given for you"* and *"shed for you* [d] *for the forgiveness of sins,"* show us that forgiveness of sin, [e] life, and salvation are given to us in the sacrament through these words, [68] because where there is forgiveness of sin, there is also life and salvation.

How can bodily eating and drinking do such a great thing? [f] Answer:
Eating and drinking certainly do not do it, but rather the words that are recorded: *"given for you"* and *"shed for you for the forgiveness of sins."* These words, when accompanied by [g] the physical eating and drinking, are the essential thing in the sacrament, and whoever believes these very words has what they declare and state, namely, *"forgiveness of sins."*

Who, then, receives this sacrament worthily? Answer:
Fasting and bodily preparation are in fact a fine external discipline, [69] but a person who has faith in these words, *"given for you"* and *"shed for you for the forgiveness of sins,"* is really worthy and well prepared. However, a person who does not believe these words or doubts them is unworthy and unprepared, because the words, *"for you,"* require truly believing hearts.

---

68. Beginning with Wittenberg's reform of liturgy in 1523 and included in the *German Mass* of 1526, the words of institution, understood as containing Jesus' testamentary promise, were chanted aloud (as opposed to the medieval practice of the priest whispering them at the altar). This practice, combined with the fact that from 1525 Wittenberg's catechisms included the words of institution as part of the "Lay Bible" to be memorized, meant that the Lord's Supper was no longer a sacrifice to be observed but a meal of God's mercy to be consumed.

69. Medieval practice required fasting before receiving the Lord's Supper. Luther distinguishes here between external preparation and the faith of the heart, which for him is not a human "work" but an action of the Holy Spirit using the gospel (see his explanation to the third article, above, p. 225).

---

c   A conflation of texts from 1 Cor. 11:23-25; Matt. 26:26-28; Mark 14:22-24; Luke 22:19f. Cf. LC, Sacrament of the Altar, par. 3 (BC, 467), and LC, Short Preface, par. 23 (BC, 385–86). This text conforms neither to the words of institution found in *The German Mass and Order of Service*, 1526 (LW 53:80–81), nor in the LC.

d   In this and the succeeding questions the words "for you," stated only once in the German, apply to both phrases.

e   Beginning with the 1536 edition of the *Small Catechism*, "sins."

f   Beginning with the 1540 edition of the *Small Catechism*, "great things."

g   German: *neben* (near, in proximity to).

How the head of the house is to teach the members of the household to say morning and evening blessings[70]

In the morning, as soon as you get out of bed, you are to make the sign of the holy cross and say:

"God the Father, Son, and Holy Spirit watch over me. Amen."

Then, kneeling or standing, say the Apostles' Creed and the Lord's Prayer. If you wish, you may in addition recite this little prayer as well:

"I give thanks to you, my heavenly Father, through Jesus Christ your dear Son, that you have protected me this night from all harm and danger, and I ask you that you would also protect me today from sin and all evil, so that my life and actions may please you completely. For into your hands I commend myself: my body, my soul, and everything else. Let your holy angel[71] be with me, so that the wicked foe may have no power over me. Amen."

After singing a hymn perhaps (for example, one on the Ten Commandments[h]) or whatever else may serve your devotion, you are to go to your work joyfully.

In the evening, when you go to bed, you are to make the sign of the holy cross and say:

"God the Father, Son, and Holy Spirit watch over me. Amen."

Then, kneeling or standing, say the Apostles' Creed and the Lord's Prayer. If you wish, you may in addition recite this little prayer as well:

"I give thanks to you, my heavenly Father, through Jesus Christ your dear Son, that you have graciously protected me today, and I ask you to forgive me all my sins, where I have done wrong, and graciously to protect me tonight. For into your hands I commend myself: my body, my soul, and everything else. Let your holy angel be with me, so that the wicked foe may have no power over me. Amen."

Then you are to go to sleep quickly and cheerfully.

70. Luther adapted this material from the Roman Breviary. The expression "say blessings" (*sich segenen*) meant in Luther's day "make the sign of the cross."

71. Luther reflects the common belief of a guardian angel for each person. See Matt. 18:10.

---

h   See LC, Short Preface, par. 24–25 (BC, 386), and Luther's own hymns on the Decalog (LW 53:277–81).

72. Here Luther uses the well-known Latin terms *benedicite* (blessing) and *gratias* (thanksgiving).

73. The material in this section was adapted from the Roman Breviary already in the 1525 Wittenberg catechism, *Das Buchlin fur die leyen und kinder* (*Booklet for the Laity and Children*), in Robert Kolb and James Nestingen, eds., *Sources and Contexts of the* Book of Concord (Minneapolis: Fortress Press, 2001), 7–8. Luther adds here instructions regarding the children's demeanor and a gloss on the word *delight*.

74. Ps. 145:15-16. The gloss that follows matches Luther's comments in his translation of the Bible about the word "pleasure" (*wohlgefallen*) connected with this text and Luke 2:14.

How the head of the house is to teach members of the household to offer blessing and thanksgiving[72] at meals[73]

[The Table Blessing][i]

The children and the members of the household are to come devoutly to the table, fold their hands and recite:

"*The eyes of all wait upon you, O* LORD, *and you give them their food at the proper time. You open your hand and satisfy all living things with delight.*"[74]

Comment: "Delight" means that all animals receive enough to eat to make them joyful and of good cheer, because worry and greed prevent such delight.

Then they are to recite the Lord's Prayer and the following prayer:

"LORD *God, heavenly Father, bless us and these your gifts, which we receive from your bountiful goodness through Jesus Christ our* LORD. *Amen.*"

Thanksgiving[j]

Similarly, after eating they should in the same manner fold their hands and recite devoutly:

"*O give thanks to the* LORD, *for he is gracious and his goodness endures forever. He gives food to all flesh. He gives food to the cattle and to the young ravens that cry to him. He takes no pleasure in the power of the horse, nor is he pleased with human strength.*[k] *The* LORD *takes pleasure in those who fear him and wait for his goodness.*"[l]

Then recite the Lord's Prayer and the following prayer:

"*We give thanks to you,* LORD *God our Father, through Jesus Christ our* LORD *for all your benefits, you who live and reign forever. Amen.*"

---

i   This title occurs only in the Latin versions: *Benedictio mensae.*

j   Luther, following the 1525 *Buchlin* (*Booklet*), uses the Latin term *gratias.*

k   German: *beinen* (legs).

l   Pss. 106:1; 136:1, 26; 147:9-11. The text follows the translations in the Luther Bible.

The Household Chart[75] of Some Bible Passages

for all kinds of holy orders[76] and walks of life,[m]
through which they may be admonished,
as through lessons particularly pertinent
to their office and duty[77]

For Bishops, Pastors, and Preachers

"A bishop is to be above reproach, the husband of one wife, temperate, virtuous, moderate, hospitable, an apt teacher, not a drunkard, not vicious, not greedy for shameless profit,[78] but gentle, not quarrelsome, not stingy, one who manages his own household well, who has obedient and honest children, not a recent convert, etc."[n] From 1 Tim. 3[:2-4, 6a].[o]

Concerning Governing Authorities

"Let everyone be subject to the governing authority. For wherever the governing authority is, it is ordered by God. But whoever resists the governing authority, resists God's order, but whoever resists will incur judgment, for that authority does not bear the sword in vain. It is God's handmaid, who executes punishment against those who do evil." From Rom. 13[:1-2, 4b].[p]

---

m German: *Stende* (stations or walks of life).

n In the 1540 edition, using a passage from Titus 1:9 inserted for "etc.": "who holds to the Word that is certain and can teach, so that he may be strong enough to admonish with saving teaching and to refute those who contradict it."

o The 1540 edition adds a section entitled "What Christians ought to do for their teachers and pastors [German: *Seelsorger*]" and includes texts from Luke 10:7; 1 Cor. 9:14; Gal. 6:6-7; 1 Tim. 5:17-18; 1 Thess. 5:12-13; and Heb. 13:17. An abbreviated form, omitting passages from Luke and 1 Thessalonians, is found in Latin translations from 1529.

p The 1542 edition adds a section entitled "What subjects ought to do for the governing authority" and includes texts from Matt. 22:21; Rom. 13:1, 5-7; 1 Tim. 2:1-2; Titus 3:1; and 1 Peter 2:13-14. An expanded form, which includes a reference to, but no text of Matt. 17:24-27, is found in Latin translations from 1529.

75. German: *Die Haustafel.* Sometimes translated "table of duties" (a meaning of the term derived from its use here), this section may have been suggested to Luther by Jean Gerson's *Tractatus de modo vivendi omnium fidelium.* Translation of the Bible passages here is based upon Luther's own rendering of the texts.

76. Luther is both criticizing the common use of this term for the monastic life and referring to the three estates: *ordo ecclesiasticus, politicus,* and *oeconomicus* (church, government, and household, respectively). See SA, Preface, par. 14, 1538 (BC, 300; TAL 2:427), and the *Confession Concerning Christ's Supper,* 1528 (LW 37:363–65). This section outlines Luther's understanding of Christian vocations in the world.

77. In his explanation of the Fourth Commandment in the *Large Catechism,* Luther detailed many of the duties outlined here. See LC, Ten Commandments, par. 103–78 (BC, 400–410; TAL 2:314-27). He also mentioned responsibilities in explanations of the Fifth through Eighth Commandments as well.

78. Influenced by a later edition of Luther's German Bible, the 1536 edition replaced "greedy for shameless profit" with "involved in dishonorable work."

79. Here Luther focuses on the household and those stations in life generally found there in the sixteenth century: husband and wife; parents and children; masters, mistresses, and workers; widows; young people.

For Husbands[79]

"You husbands, live reasonably with your wives and give honor, as coheirs of the grace of life, to wives as to the weak[q] instrument, so that your prayers may not be hindered." From 1 Peter 3[:7]. "And do not be harsh with them." From Col. 3[:19].

For Wives

"Let wives be subjected to their husbands as to the LORD, as Sarah obeyed Abraham and called him lord. And you have become her daughters, when you do right and are not afraid of any terrifying thing."[r] From 1 Peter 3[:1, 6].[80]

80. The words "as to the LORD" come from Eph. 5:22.

For Parents

"You fathers, do not provoke your children to anger, lest they become fearful. Instead, bring them up in the discipline and admonition of the LORD." From Eph. 6[:4].

For Children

"You children, be obedient to your parents in the LORD, for this is right. 'Honor your father and mother.' This is the first commandment that has a promise, namely: 'that it may go well for you and that you may live long on earth.'" From Eph. 6[:1-3].

For Male and Female Servants, Day Laborers, Workers, and the Like

81. German: *Knechte* (the male servant in the German household).

"You servants,[81] be obedient to your bodily lords with fear and trembling, with singleness of heart, as to Christ himself; not with service meant only for the eyes, done to please people, but rather as servants of Christ, so that you do the will of God from the heart with compliance.[s] Imagine to yourselves that you are

---

q   Beginning in the 1536 version: "weakest."

r   The 1536 edition replaced "afraid of any terrifying thing" with "so fearful." See LW 30:87–91 for Luther's sermon on this text from 1522.

s   The 1536 version, following later editions of the Wittenberg translation of the Bible, reads "with a good will."

serving the LORD and not people, and know that whatever good anyone does, the same will that person receive, whether a servant or free."[t]

For Masters and Mistresses[82]

"You masters, do the same to them, and refrain from making threats, and know that you also have a Lord in heaven, and there is no partiality with him."[u]

For Young People in General

"You young people, be subject to your elders and in this way show humility. For 'God opposes the proud but gives grace to the humble.' Therefore humble yourselves under the mighty hand of God, so that he may exalt you in his time." From 1 Peter 5[:5-6].

For Widows

"She who is a real widow and is left all alone sets her hope on God and remains in prayer day and night; whereas she who lives self-indulgently is dead while alive." From 1 Tim. 5[:5-6].

For All in the Community[83]

"Love your neighbor as yourself. In this all the commandments are summarized." From Rom. 13[:9]. "And continually entreat [God] with prayers for all people." From 1 Tim. 2[:1].[v]

Let all their lessons learn with care,
So that the household well may fare.[84]

82. German: *Hausherrn und Hausfrauen*: literally, "the lords and ladies of the house," that is, the heads of households.

83. German: *der Gemeine*. This word may be translated the congregation, the community, or all in common. See *Confession Concerning Christ's Supper*, 1528 (LW 37:367–68).

84. This is most likely Luther's own rhyme. See WA 35:580.

---

t   From Eph. 6:5-8.
u   The 1536 version adds: "Eph. 6[:9]."
v   A loose paraphrase.

1536 section title: "Marriage
Booklet for Simple Pastors"

A Marriage Booklet for Simple Pastors[85]

Martin Luther

"So many lands, so many customs," says the common adage.
For this reason, because weddings and the married estate are
worldly affairs, it behooves those of us who are "spirituals"[86] or
ministers of the church in no way to order or direct anything
regarding marriage, but instead to allow every city and land to
continue their own customs and practices that are now in use.
Some bring the bride to the church twice, in both the evening
and the morning; some only once. Some announce it publicly
and publish the banns from the pulpit two or three weeks in
advance. All these and similar things I leave to the prince and
town council to create and arrange as they want. It is no concern
of mine.[87]

However, when people request of us to bless them in front of
the church or in the church, to pray over them, or even to marry
them, we are obligated to do this. Therefore I wanted to offer
these words of advice and this order for those who do not know
anything better, in case they are inclined to use this common
order with us. Others, who can do better (that is, who can do
nothing at all and who nevertheless think they know it all), do

not need this service of mine, unless they might greatly improve on it and masterfully correct it. They certainly ought to take great care not to follow the same practice as others. A person might think that they had learned something from someone else! That would be a real shame!

Because up to now people have made such an impressive, great display at the consecrations of monks and nuns (even though their station in life[w] and existence is an ungodly, human invention without any basis in the Bible), how much more should we honor this godly station of marriage and bless it, pray for it, and adorn it in an even more glorious manner. For, although it is a worldly station, nevertheless it has God's Word on its side and is not a human invention or institution, like the station of monks and nuns.[88] Therefore it should easily be reckoned a hundred times more spiritual than the monastic station, which certainly ought to be considered the most worldly and fleshly of all, because it was invented and instituted by flesh and blood and completely out of a worldly understanding and reason.

We must also do this in order that the young people may learn to take this station in life seriously, to hold it in high esteem as a divine work and command, and not to ridicule it in such outrageous ways with laughing, jeering, and similar levity. This has been common until now, as if it were a joke or child's play to get married or to hold a wedding. Those who first instituted the custom of bringing a bride and bridegroom to church surely did not view it as a joke but as a very serious matter.[x] For there is no doubt that they wanted thereby to receive God's blessing and the community's[89] prayers and not put on a comedy or a pagan farce.

The ceremony itself makes this clear. For all[y] who desire prayer and blessing from the pastor or bishop[90] indicate thereby—whether or not they say so expressly—to what danger and need they are exposing themselves and how much they need God's blessing and the community's prayers for the station of life into which they are entering. For they experience every day how much

88. For a similar criticism see also *The Estate of Marriage*, 1522 (LW 45:17–49), and *The Judgment of Martin Luther on Monastic Vows*, 1521 (LW 44:245–400).

89. Luther is thinking of the general prayers for the couple made by the community in worship.

90. Luther understood that the chief pastor in a town was its bishop. For example, see *Lectures on 1 Timothy*, 1528 (LW 28:281–84); *Answer to the Hyperchristian . . . Book*, 1521 (LW 39:154–56); and *Instruction by the Visitors*, 1528 (LW 40:269–71); as well as the SC, Preface, and Household Chart, above, pp. 212 and 239.

---

w Here and throughout this tract, the German word *Stand* is translated "station of life" or "walk of life." In older translations it was rendered "estate."

x See Luther's *Sermon at Marriage of Sigismund von Lindenau*, 1545 (LW 51:363–64).

y Singular in the original.

unhappiness the devil causes in the marital station through adultery, unfaithfulness, discord, and all kinds of misery.

Therefore we want to deal with the bride and bridegroom (when they desire and demand it) in the following way.

First, publish the banns[91] from the pulpit with the following words:

"John N. and Mary N.[92] wish to enter the holy station of matrimony according to God's ordinance and desire the common Christian prayers[93] on their behalf so that they may begin it in God's name and have it turn out well.

Now should anyone have anything to say against this, let him or her speak at this time or hereafter remain silent. God grant them his blessing. AMEN."

Exchange vows[94] in front of the church with the following words:

"John, do you desire to have Mary as your wedded wife?"
Let him answer[z]: "Yes."
"Mary, do you desire to have John as your wedded husband?"
Let her answer: "Yes."

At this point let them exchange wedding rings and join their right hands together, and say to them:
What God joins together, no human being ought to separate."[a]

Then let the pastor declare to all who are present:
"Therefore, because John N. and Mary N. desire each other in marriage and confess the same here publicly in the presence of God and the world, in testimony of which they have given each other their hands and wedding rings, I pronounce them joined in marriage, in the name of the Father, and of the Son, and of the Holy Spirit. Amen."

In front of the altar[95] let the pastor read God's word from Gen. 2[:18, 21-24] over the bride and groom.

91. The "banns" were a legal declaration, usually made by the pastor, announcing the impending marriage of a couple and asking the community to express grounds why the marriage should not take place (usually because of a previous marriage or betrothal). For Luther's opinion of betrothals, a source of much debate in the sixteenth century, see *On Marriage Matters*, 1530 (LW 46:290–91).

92. German: *Hans und Greta*, common names for a couple, but also the names of Luther's own parents.

93. That is, the general prayers made in worship.

94. Luther believed that marriage should follow soon after betrothal. Because the exchange of vows was considered a matter of civil law, it took place at the door of the church.

95. This marks the beginning of the worship service.

---

z　　Here and below Luther employs the standard Latin term *dicat*.
a　　Matt. 19:6.

"*Then the* LORD *God said, 'It is not good that the human being should be alone; I will make him a helper who will be his companion.'*[b] *So the* LORD *God caused a deep sleep to fall upon the human being, and he slept; and he took one of his ribs and closed up its place with flesh. And the* LORD *God built a woman out of the rib that he had taken from the human being, and he brought her to him. Then the human being said: 'This is truly bone of my bone and flesh of my flesh. This one will be called woman, because she is taken out of man.' Therefore a man will leave his father and mother and cling to his wife, and the two will be one flesh.*"

Then let the pastor turn to both and address them thus:

"Because you both have entered into the married estate in God's name, hear first of all God's commandment concerning this estate. Thus says St. Paul:[c]

"'*Husbands, love your wives, just as Christ loved the congregation*[d] *and gave himself up for it, in order to make it holy, and has cleansed it through the washing of water in the Word, in order to present for himself a glorious congregation,*[e] *that has neither spot nor wrinkle nor anything of the kind, but instead so that it may be holy and blameless. So also husbands ought to love their wives like their own bodies. He who loves his wife loves himself. For no one ever hated his own flesh, but instead he nourishes it and takes care of it, just as the* LORD *does for the congregation.*

"'*Wives, be subject to your husbands as to the* LORD*. For the husband is the head of the wife, just as Christ is also the head of the congregation, and he is the savior of his body. But as now the congregation is subject to Christ, so also the women are subject to their husbands in all things.'*

"Second, hear also the cross that God has placed upon this station.[f]

---

b   The 1536 version corresponds to the complete edition of the Luther Bible from 1534: "who will stand by his side."

c   Eph. 5:25-29, 22-24.

d   German: *Gemeine* (congregation or community), following the translation of Luther's German translation, the *September Testament* of 1522.

e   The 1536 version corresponds to the complete edition of Luther's 1534 translation of the Bible: "prepare for himself a community that will be glorious."

f   Gen. 3:16-19.

96. The following prayer is an adaptation of a traditional prayer used at nuptial Masses in Luther's day.

97. German: *Kirchen*. Luther did not view marriage as a sacrament but uses the word here as found in the traditional prayer to refer to Eph. 5:32, where the Vulgate translates the Greek *mystērion* with *sacramentum*. See LW 36:92–95. In the gloss on this text in the 1522 translation of the New Testament (WA Bi 7:206), Luther states, "'*geheymnis*: *sacramentum* or *mysterion* means secret [*geheymnis*] or a hidden thing, which nevertheless has its own signification. Thus, Christ and his congregation is a secret, that is, a great, holy, hidden thing, that one must believe and cannot see. It is signified by a man and wife, as by an external sign; that just as a man and wife are one body and hold all property in common, so also the congregation has everything that Christ is and has.'"

98. The *Baptismal Booklet*, based upon medieval baptismal rites, was originally published in 1523 (LW 53:95–103). In 1526 a second edition was prepared (LW 53:106–9 with 101–3), which is the basis of the translation here. It was included in the second edition of the *Small Catechism* published in 1529, in all subsequent editions published in Wittenberg during Luther's lifetime, and in some editions of the *Book of Concord*. The rite shows Luther's deep respect for the liturgical tradition, his connection between baptism and the defeat of evil, and his insistence that the promises bestowed in baptism were a lifelong gift from God. Moreover, as his introduction made clear, Luther refocused the liturgical action on the actual baptizing with water, as opposed to the other practices that surrounded it.

"'To the woman God said:

"'"*I will create much distress for you in childbirth. You shall bear your children in distress, and you shall cringe before your husband, and he shall be your lord.*"

"'And to the man God said:

"'"*Because you have listened to the voice of your wife and have eaten from the tree, about which I commanded you and said, 'You shall not eat from it,' cursed is the ground because of you. In distress you shall nourish yourself your whole life long. The ground shall bring forth thorns and thistles for you, and you shall eat the plants of the field. By the sweat of your face shall you eat your bread, until you return again to the earth from which you were taken. For you are earth and shall return to earth.*"'

"Third, this is your comfort, that you know and believe how your estate is pleasing and blessed in God's eyes. For it is written:[g]

"'*God created human beings in his image, in the image of God he created them. He created them a male and a female, and God blessed them and said to them: "Be fruitful and multiply, and fill the earth and bring it under your control; and have dominion over the fish in the sea and over the birds in the air and over all animals that crawl on the earth." And God saw all that he had made, and look, it was all very good.*'

"Therefore Solomon also says,[h]

"'*Whoever gets a wife, gets a good thing and will obtain delight from the* LORD.'"

At this point let the pastor spread his hands over them and pray:[96]

"LORD *God, who have created man and woman and have ordained them for the station of marriage, have blessed them also with the fruit of the womb, and have therein signified the sacrament of your dear Son, Jesus Christ, and the church,[97] his bride: We beseech your never-ending goodness that you would not permit this your creation, ordinance, and blessing to be removed or destroyed, but graciously preserve it among us through Jesus Christ our* LORD. *AMEN.*"

---

g   Gen. 1:27-28, 31.

h   A paraphrase of Prov. 18:22. The 1536 version reads, "Whoever finds a wife, finds a good thing and obtains a blessing from the LORD."

1536 section title: *The Baptismal Booklet: Translated into German and Newly Revised*

99. In the Roman rite only the questions to the sponsors and their responses were not in Latin.

100. German: *ernstlich.* Throughout this preface, Luther repeatedly uses this adverb and other forms of the word, which is translated here either "earnestly" or "seriously."

101. German: *Kinder heben,* literally, "to draw children out of the font." See the order of service below. The sponsors are to hold the child over the font while the priest puts on the christening robe.

The Baptismal Booklet:
Translated into German and Newly Revised[98]

Martin Luther

To all Christian readers: Grace and peace in Christ our Lord. Because daily I see and hear with what carelessness and lack of solemnity—to say nothing of out and out levity—people[i] treat the high, holy, and comforting Sacrament of Baptism for infants, in part caused, I believe, by the fact that those present understand nothing of what is being said and done, I have decided that it is not only helpful but also necessary to conduct the service in the German language. For this reason I have attempted to translate these things[99] in order to begin baptizing in German, so that the sponsors and others present may all the more be aroused to faith and earnest[100] devotion and so that the priests who baptize have to show more diligence for the sake of the listeners.

Out of a sense of Christian commitment, I appeal to all those who baptize, sponsor infants,[101] or witness a baptism to take to

1536 caption: "The figure: Matthew 28:16-20." See also the caption for this image on p. 230.

---

i   Singular in the original.

heart the tremendous work and great earnestness present here. For here in the words of these prayers you hear how plaintively and earnestly the Christian church brings the infant here, confesses before God with such steadfast, undoubting words that the infant is possessed by the devil and a child of sin and perniciousness, and through baptism so diligently asks for help and grace, so that the infant may become a child of God.

Therefore, you have to realize that it is no joke at all to take action against the devil and not only drive him away from the little child but also hang around the child's neck such a mighty, lifelong enemy. For this reason, it is absolutely necessary to stand by the poor child with all one's heart and with a strong faith and to plead with great devotion that God, in accordance with these prayers, would not only free the child from the devil's power but also strengthen the child, so that the child might resist him valiantly[j] in life and in death. I fear that people turn out so badly after baptism because we have dealt with them in such a cold and casual way and have not prayed at all earnestly for them at their baptism.

Bear in mind, too, that in baptism the external ceremonies are least important, such as blowing under the eyes, making the sign of the cross, putting salt in the mouth or spit and clay in the ears and nose, anointing the breast and shoulders with oil, smearing the head with chrism, putting on the christening robe, placing a burning candle in the person's hand, and whatever else has been added by humans to embellish baptism.[102] For certainly a baptism can occur without any of these things, and they are not the actual devices from which the devil shrinks or flees. He sneers at even greater things than these! Here things must get really serious.

Instead, see to it that you are present there in true faith, that you listen to God's word, and that you pray along earnestly.[103] For wherever the priest says, "Let us pray," he is exhorting you to pray with him. Moreover, all sponsors and the others present ought to speak along with him the words of his prayer in their hearts to God. For this reason, the priest should speak these prayers very clearly and slowly, so that the sponsors can hear and understand them and can also pray with the priest with one mind in their hearts, carrying before God the need of the little child with all

102. Many of these practices go back to the rites for baptismal preparation and baptism used in the ancient church, which in turn reflected the actions of Christ in healing the blind and deaf, or the anointing of priests and kings from the Old Testament, or imagery from Paul's letters. See, for example, Mark 7:33; Mark 8:23; Exod. 29:7; 1 Sam. 10:1; and Gal. 3:27. Others reflect the sayings of Christ about Christians as the salt of the earth and light of the world (Matt. 5:13-16).

103. For Luther, prayer was no longer simply holy words that were effective merely by their being spoken (*ex opere operato*), but truly begging God to act, in this case, on behalf of the baptizand. For more on his condemnation of "useless howling and growling" see the LC, Lord's Prayer, par. 4–34 (BC, 441–45, here 444, par. 33).

---

j   German: *ritterlich*, literally, "chivalrously," "like a knight."

earnestness, on the child's behalf setting themselves against the devil with all their strength, and demonstrating that they take seriously what is no joke to the devil.

For this reason it is absolutely right and proper not to allow drunken and boorish clerics[k] to baptize nor to select good-for-nothings as godparents. Instead fine, moral, serious, upright priests and godparents ought to be chosen, who can be expected to treat the matter with seriousness and true faith, lest this high sacrament be abandoned to the devil's mockery and dishonor God, who in this sacrament showers upon us the vast and boundless riches of his grace. He himself calls it a "new birth,"[l] through which we, being freed from the devil's tyranny and loosed from sin, death, and hell, become children of life, heirs of all God's possessions, God's own children, and Christ's brothers and sisters.[m]

Ah, dear Christians, let us not value or treat this unspeakable gift so half-heartedly. For baptism is our only comfort, the entrance into all of God's possessions, and communion with all the saints. To this end may God help us! AMEN.

The Baptizer shall say:
"Depart, you unclean spirit, and make room for the Holy Spirit."

Then he shall make the sign of the cross on both the forehead and the breast and say:
"Receive the sign of the holy cross upon the forehead and the breast.

"Let us pray.
"O almighty and eternal God, Father of our Lord Jesus Christ, I call to you on behalf of this, your servant, N., who asks for the gift of your baptism and desires your eternal grace through spiritual rebirth.

"Receive him,"[n] Lord, and as you have said, 'Ask and you shall receive, seek and you shall find, knock and it shall be open for you,'[o] so give now the blessing to him who asks and open the door to him who knocks on it, so

---

k   German: *Pfaffen*, often used by Luther in a negative sense.

l   John 3:3, 5.

m   Literally: "brethren."

n   Throughout Luther uses the masculine pronoun for the one being baptized.

o   Matt. 7:7.

that he may obtain the eternal blessing of this heavenly bath[p] and receive the promised kingdom you give through Christ our Lord. Amen.

"Let us pray:

"Almighty, eternal God, who according to your strict judgment condemned the unbelieving world through the flood and according to your great mercy preserved believing Noah and the seven members of his family, and who drowned hardhearted Pharaoh with his army in the Red Sea and led your people Israel through the same sea on dry ground, thereby prefiguring this bath of your Holy Baptism, and who through the baptism of your dear child, our Lord Jesus Christ, hallowed and set apart the Jordan and all water to be a blessed flood and a rich washing away of sins: we ask that through this very same boundless mercy of yours you would look graciously upon N. and in the [Holy] Spirit bless him with true faith[q] so that through this saving flood all that has been born in him from Adam and whatever he has added thereto may be drowned in him and perish, and that he, separated from the number of the unbelieving, may be preserved dry and secure in the holy ark of the Christian Church and may at all times, fervent in spirit and joyful in hope, serve your name, so that with all believers in your promise he may become worthy to attain eternal life through Jesus Christ our Lord. Amen.

"I adjure you, you unclean spirit, in the name of the Father (+) and of the Son (+) and of the Holy Spirit (+), that you come out of and depart from this servant of Jesus Christ, N. AMEN.

"Let us hear the holy Gospel of St. Mark:[104, 105]

"'At that time, they brought little children to Jesus that he might touch them. But the disciples threatened[r] those who brought them. But when Jesus saw this, he became annoyed with them and said to them, "Let the little children come to me and do not prevent them. For of such is the kingdom of God. Truly, I say to you, whoever does not receive the kingdom of God like a little child will not enter into it." And he hugged them and laid his hands on them and blessed them.'"

Then the priest shall lay his hands upon the child's head and pray the Lord's Prayer along with the kneeling sponsors:

104. Mark 10:13-16. First with the 1536 edition does the text match the Luther Bible. Until then the text in the *Small Catechism* represented a free rendering of the text, perhaps based upon the Latin Vulgate.

105. This story came to be depicted in paintings often hung near the font, many of which were executed by Lucas Cranach the Elder. Such images served as an important visual reminder of Lutheran baptismal practices over against those who denied the efficacy of infant baptism.

p   See Titus 3:5.
q   Or: "bless him with true faith in the spirit."
r   The 1536 edition reads: "led away."

"*Our Father, you who are in heaven, hallowed be your name, may your kingdom come, may your will come about as in heaven, so, too, on earth. Give us today our daily bread. And forgive us our debts as we forgive our debtors. And lead us not into temptation, but deliver us from evil. Amen.*"

After this the little child shall be brought to the baptismal font[106] and the priest shall say:

"*The* LORD *preserve your coming in and your going out from now and for evermore.*"[s]

Jesus blesses the children (Mark 10:13-16), by Lucas Cranach the Elder. The importance of this text for baptisms led the artist and his son to produce many oil paintings of this scene to hang near baptismal fonts in Lutheran churches.

Then the priest shall let the child through his sponsors renounce the devil and say:

"*N., do you renounce the devil?*"
Answer: "Yes."
"*And all his works?*"
Answer: "Yes."
"*And all his ways?*"
Answer: "Yes."
Then he shall ask:
"*Do you believe in God the Father almighty, creator of heaven and earth?*"
Answer: "Yes."
"*Do you believe in Jesus Christ, his only Son our Lord, who was born and suffered?*"
Answer: "Yes."

106. According to the medieval rite, the exorcisms took place at the door of the church and the rest of the service at the baptismal font.

s   Ps. 121:8.

"Do you believe in the Holy Spirit, one holy Christian church, the communion of saints, [t] *forgiveness of sins, resurrection of the body, and after death an eternal life?"*

Answer: "Yes."

"Do you want to be baptized?"

Answer: "Yes."

At this point he shall take the child and immerse[u] it in the baptismal font and say:

"And I baptize you in the name of the Father and of the Son and of the Holy Spirit."

Then the sponsors shall hold the little child over the font, and the priest, while putting the christening robe on the child, shall say:

"The almighty God and Father of our LORD *Jesus Christ, who has given birth to you for a second time through water and the Holy Spirit and has forgiven you all your sins, strengthen you with his grace to eternal life. Amen."*

"Peace be with you."

Answer: "AMEN."

Printed in Wittenberg by Nicholas Schirlentz
1531[107]

107. Various editions of the *Small Catechism* also add other material. Editions published in Wittenberg during Luther's lifetime included in 1529: *The German Litany* (LW 53:163–69); in 1536, 1537, and 1539: the German *Te Deum* and *Magnificat* (LW 53:171–79); in 1543: "A Prayer against the Turks" (LW 43:232–33).

t   German: *Gemeine der heiligen*, literally, "community of the holy ones."
u   German: *tauchen* (immerse or dip).

Image Credits